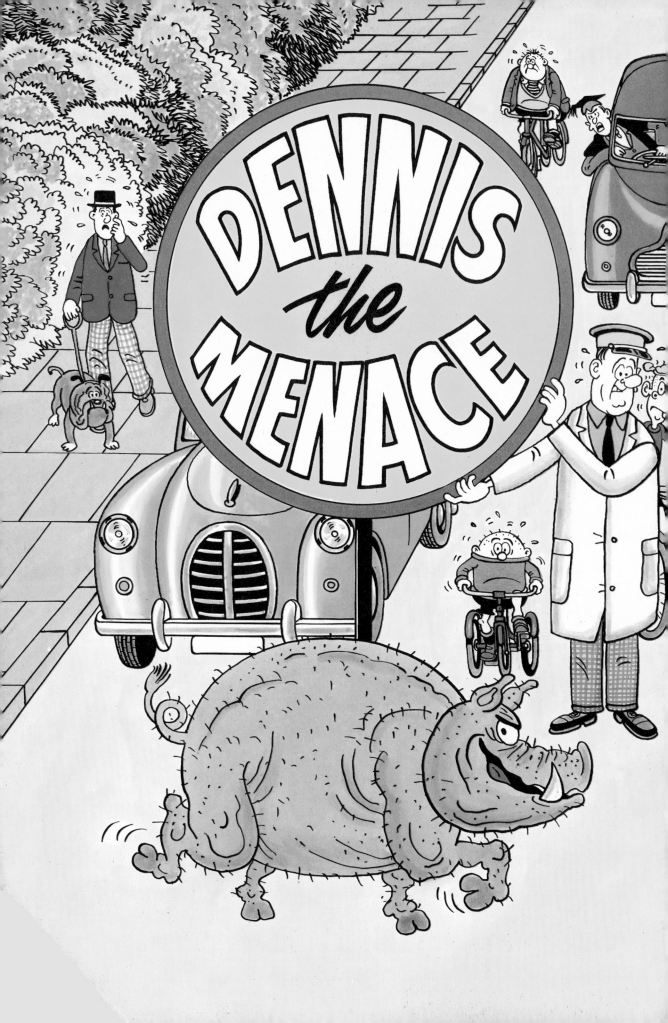

and GNASHER

1983

Printed and Published in Great Britain by D.C. THOMSON & CO., LTD.,
185 Fleet Street, London, EC4A 2'HS. © D.C. THOMSON & CO., LTD., 1982.
ISBN 0 85116 263 0

HAIR TODAY, GONE TOMORROW

PULLOVER PALAVER

What A Howl!

EEK! WHAT'S THAT?

HOWL! SCREECH! YEEOW!

HMPH! SOUNDS AS IF THAT MENACE BOY IS BEING UNKIND TO THAT POOR LITTLE DOG OF HIS!

MRS PODGER, LOCAL BUSYBODY.

SO—

I REPRESENT THE KINDNESS TO ANIMALS COMMITTEE, AND I HAVE REASON TO BELIEVE THAT DENNIS HAS BEEN UNKIND TO HIS DOG!

DO HAVE A SEAT, MRS PODGER. I'LL CALL DENNIS.

THEN—
THIS IS MRS PODGER FROM THE KINDNESS TO ANIMALS COMMITTEE. SHE WANTS TO HAVE A WORD WITH YOU:

IF MRS PODGER'S SO KIND TO ANIMALS, WHY IS SHE SITTING ON MY PET FROG?

WHAT?

YOU OK, FRED?

CROAK!

SHRIEK!

FOND MAMA

WE'RE ALL THE BEST OF PALS! I WOULDN'T BE UNKIND TO MY PETS!

UT WHAT WAS ALL THAT HOWLING THAT MRS PODGER HEARD?

OH, I WAS JUST GIVING GNASHER SOME SINGING LESSONS!

1-2-3-

—BEGIN!

WELL, MAYBE HE WASN'T UNKIND TO ANIMALS—BUT THIS IS CERTAINLY UNKIND TO EARDRUMS!

YOWOOO! YOWEE!

CROOAK! CROAK!

BIG GAME HUNTER

DISAPPEARING

SPORTS SCENE

BRICK TRICK

THINGS ARE LOOKING BLACK

COO! COMMANDOS USED BLACK DYE TO DISGUISE THEMSELVES AT NIGHT!

CAN I HAVE SOME BLACK SHOE POLISH, MUM?

CERTAINLY, DENNIS! I'M GLAD TO SEE YOU'RE GOING TO CLEAN YOUR SHOES AT LAST.

BUT—

I'LL BE JUST LIKE A COMMANDO!

LATER—

TCH! TCH! TOM'S LEFT HIS CART PARKED ON A DOUBLE YELLOW LINE.

I MUST GET HIM HIM TO MOVE HIS CART—EEK!

PING!

ZIP!

AT DENNIS'S HOUSE —

IT HAD TO BE DENNIS—BUT I COULDN'T SEE HIM ANYWHERE!

I'LL CHECK HIS USUAL HIDING PLACES.

COAL CELLAR

HM! NO SIGN OF HIM IN THERE.

BUT—

WHAT'S THIS?—AHA! I'M BEGINNING TO UNDERSTAND!

COMMANDO TACTIC 3. FACE BLACKENING

I'LL BORROW A WATER PISTOL AND SOME LUMINOUS PAINT FROM DENNIS'S TOY BOX.

DENNISS TOY BOX

LUMINOUS PAINT

THEN—

AHA!

SPRAY—

THIS PICTURE HAS BEEN BLACKENED OUT TO SAVE OUR READERS FROM WITNESSING AN UNHAPPY EVENT—

MAKING SPARKS FLY

LOCAL VET. IS GIVING AN ANIMAL-CARE LECTURE —

A NICE BIG BONE IS VERY GOOD FOR YOUR DOG'S TEETH.

HEAR THAT, GNASHER?

GNASH!

SO —

HERE, GNASHER!

BUTCHER

HUH! THAT DIDN'T LAST LONG!

CRUNCH!
CRACK!
SPLINTER!

IN THE PET SHOP—

EXTRA-TOUGH
MEATY FLAVOUR
PLASTIC BONE

TRY THIS FOR SIZE, GNASHER!

GRIND!
CHUMP!
MASH!

GULP! GNASHER'S TURNED THE EXTRA-TOUGH BONE INTO A HEAP OF POWDER!

GASP!

NOD

AT THE BLACKSMITH'S —

COULD YOU MAKE ME A SOLID STEEL BONE, MR BLACKSMITH?

SURE!

LATER—

THIS'LL TICKLE GNASHER'S TONSILS!

MEAT PASTE

SOLID STEEL BONE

THAT'LL KEEP HIM CHEWING FOR A WHILE!

GNASHER

SPARK
GNASH!
CLANK!

LATER—

HEY, MR VET., YOU SAID BONES WERE GOOD FOR DOGS—BUT MY DOG CAUGHT A COLD THROUGH CHEWING A BONE!

GOOD GRACIOUS, MY BOY! HOW COULD THAT POSSIBLY HAPPEN?

GNASHOO!

GNASHER SET FIRE TO HIS KENNEL BY CHEWING HIS BONE—HE WAS OUT ALL NIGHT IN THE DAMP AIR!

ASTONISHING!

SNIFF!
SNIFF!

SPACE INVADERS

...DOG TRAVELS ROUND MOON...MEN LAND ON MOON! COO! WE MUST TRY TO JOIN IN THE SPACE RACE, GNASHER!

HISTORY OF SPACE TRAVEL

SO. DENNIS PUTS ON HIS TOY SPACE-SUIT—

COO! WALTER'S GOT A SPACE-SUIT, TOO!

I'LL GET MY PET MOUSE TO ASK WALTER IF HE'LL LEND GNASHER HIS SPACE-SUIT!

PLOP!

SHRIEK! IT'S A HORRIBLE MOUSE!

THANKS FOR LENDING US THE SPACE-SUIT, WALTER.

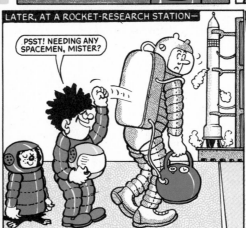

LATER, AT A ROCKET-RESEARCH STATION—

PSST! NEEDING ANY SPACEMEN, MISTER?

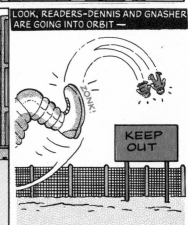

LOOK, READERS—DENNIS AND GNASHER ARE GOING INTO ORBIT—

ZONK!

KEEP OUT

I'LL JUST HAVE TO MAKE MY OWN ROCKETSHIP. THIS BIN'LL MAKE A FINE CAPSULE.

JUST GET RID OF THE RUBBISH FIRST.

HOWL!

OOER! HELLO, DAD! FANCY SEEING YOU HERE!

GRR! SNARL! WAIT TILL I GET MY SLIPPER!

WATCH THIS SPACE

ZOOM

LOOK, READERS— DENNIS IS LEADING IN THIS SPACE RACE!

BUT DAD CATCHES UP—

ONE GOOD THING ABOUT SPACE HELMETS —THEY KEEP THE YELLS DOWN!

QUIET OOYAH!

SILENT HOWL!

HOW VERY

EGGS"ASPERATING

LOOK at the LOLLY!

LOVELY! MY NEW FRIDGE HAS ARRIVED!

COO! I CAN KEEP SNOW-BALLS IN IT IN SUMMER!

LATER —

DENNIS! GNASHER! I'VE A SURPRISE FOR YOU!

ICE LOLLIES — MADE WITH FROZEN LEMONADE!

COO! TA, MUM!

GNASH! TA!

SLURP! IT MUST BE VERY EASY TO MAKE AN ICE LOLLY!

SO —

ALL I NEED IS A BIG PLASTIC BUCKET —

— AND A BROOM HANDLE!

CLUNK!

DAD WON'T MIND MY BORROWING HIS SUPPLY OF POP!

HALF AN HOUR LATER —

THE BIGGEST ICE LOLLY IN THE WORLD! SLURP!

THEN —

AH! I ALWAYS LIKE THE CLEAR LEMONADE BEST.

THIRSTY

POP'S POP

GURR! THESE BOTTLES ARE EMPTY — AND I CAN GUESS WHO'S EMPTIED THEM!

POP

HOW DARE YOU GLUG ALL MY LEMONADE? BEND OVER!

POP

ONE WHACKING LATER —

WHEW! THIS LOLLY IS PERFECT FOR COOLING ME DOWN!

SILENT MIRTH

SSSS FIZZZ

ON THE WRONG TRACK

CLATTER! RATTLE!

INTO THE TUNNEL—

TRUNDLE!

THEN—

PAH! STOP SLEEPING ACROSS MY MODEL RAILWAY LINE, GNASHER!

I WANT TO BE AN ENGINE DRIVER WHEN I GROW UP, LIKE MY UNCLE JOHN.

POLISH

LATER —AND DENNIS AND JOHN WILL BE HANDLING THE TRAIN TOGETHER!

COO!

YAHOO! MY UNCLE JOHN MUST BE TAKING ME FOR A TRIP ON HIS TRAIN!

LITTLE ENGINE DRIVER OUTFIT

HELLO, UNCLE JOHN! WHEN DO I GET MY HANDS ON THIS TRAIN?

YOU'RE GOING IN THE WRONG DIRECTION MY BOY!

LATER—

BAH! THEY WANTED ME TO HANDLE THE BRIDE'S TRAIN AT COUSIN NELLIES WEDDING!

HOW SWEET!

LITTLE COUSIN JOHN

YOU'VE BEEN A GOOD BOY TODAY, DENNIS! YOU CAN COME FOR A RIDE ON MY TRAIN TOMORROW!

COO! THANKS, UNCLE JOHN!

MUSICAL MENACE

DENNIS AND HIS PALS ARE PLAYING AT "KNIGHTS OF OLDE"—

ON GUARD, SIR DENALOT!

HAVE AT YE, SIR WALTER!

ON GUARD, YOU SCURVY DOG!

THEN—

COME WITH ME, SIR DENALOT! TIME FOR YOU TO FACE THE MUSIC!

NOW, DO AT LEAST AN HOUR'S PRACTICE!

HORRIBLE DIN

TINGLE! TANGLE!

HERE, GNASHER!

HM! THE PLAYING'S IMPROVED— THERE'S SOMETHING FISHY GOING ON!

AND—

WHAT'S THE MEANING OF THIS?

AW, MUM, I'M FED UP OF PIANO PLAYING! I WISH I'D LIVED IN THE OLD DAYS AND BEEN A PAGE-BOY TO SIR LANCELOT.

KNIGHTS OF OLDE

IT MUST HAVE BEEN GREAT TO LIVE IN THE GOLDEN DAYS—PLENTY OF JOUSTING AND SO ON!

THEATRE

PAGE-BOY WANTED — APPLY WITHIN →

OH, BOY! JUST THE JOB FOR ME!

MUST GET INTO MY PAGE-BOY OUTFIT!

FOOTBALL SHORTS

FOOTBALL STOCKINGS

NOW TO COMB MY HAIR INTO A "PAGE-BOY BOB."

AT THE THEATRE—

ONE PAGE-BOY REPORTING!

I SUPPOSE YOU'LL HAVE TO DO—NOBODY ELSE HAS APPLIED!

LATER—

BEETROOT'S UNFINISHED SYMPHONY (LASTS 7 HOURS)

BAH! THEY WANTED A BOY TO TURN THE PAGES OF MUSIC—AND I WANTED TO GET AWAY FROM PIANO PLAYING!

TINKLE!

TINKLE!

IN NEED of a LEAD!

IN THE PARK—

BOING!

CAN'T YOU TWO READ? NO DOGS ALLOWED, EXCEPT ON A LEAD!

JAB

NO DOGS ALLOWED EXCEPT ON LEAD

SO—

MUM WON'T MIND MY BORROWING HER CLOTHES ROPE!

KEEP OFF THE GRASS

BUT—

ERK!

GET A SHORTER LEAD!

KEEP OFF EVERYTHING

GNASH!

SO—

THAT'S BETTER!

WHOOPS! PERHAPS I SHOULDN'T HAVE USED DAD'S ELASTIC BELT AS A LEAD!

STRE-E-ETCH

GNASH! GNASH!

MEOW!

VOING!

YIPSH!

GRR! WHERE'S THAT PESKY DOG?

DOG? WHAT DOG?

GURR! HERE IT IS!

OOPS!

IN THE PET SHOP—

I'LL HAVE TWO OF THESE!

REAL LEATHER COLLAR AND LEAD

I DIDN'T KNOW YOU'D GOT ANOTHER DOG.

DOGGIE BISCUITS

LATER—

HO-HO! IT'S A PLEASURE TO MEET ONE OF OUR LEADING CITIZENS!

DOUBLE TROUBLE

RUNAWAY RASCAL

PAINTING

I'M GLAD YOU'RE HERE, DENNIS! YOU CAN HELP ME PAINT THESE WALLS!

W-WHAT?

G-GNAT?

CHUCKLE! THAT'S GOT RID OF THEM! NOW I CAN WORK IN PEACE!

SLAM!

GROAN! I'VE BEEN SENT A TIN OF PINK PAINT INSTEAD OF YELLOW. AH, WELL! IT'LL JUST HAVE TO BE THE SAME COLOUR ON THE WALLS AGAIN.

LATER —

THAT GAME WAS FUN. LET'S SEE DAD GOT ON WITHOUT US! TEE-H

EEK! MY NEWLY-PAINTED WALL!

Dennis was here

NEWLY-PAINTED WALL? GULP!

TOMORROW, YOU'LL GET MORE PAINT WITH YOUR POCKET MONEY, AND REPAINT THIS ROOM.

Y-YES, DAD!

THAT NIGHT —

NOW TO BURGLE THIS HOUSE!

FLY CAPERS

ZOOM!

ALL'S SAFE, 'ASHER.

HUH! DAD HASN'T DONE ANY PAINTING AT ALL. IT'S STILL THE SAME COLOUR. LET'S HAVE SOME FUN!

LATER—

I'LL SEE IF THE PAINT'S DRIED.

SAVE ME FROM THAT 'ORRIBLE HORROR—

THEN—

IS THAT THE POLICE? WELL, I HEARD THIS SCREAM AND FOUND A BURGLAR HAD FAINTED IN OUR FRONT ROOM—A REWARD? HOW NICE!

NEXT MORNING—

YES, DAD. WITH THIS HALF OF THE REWARD, I'LL GET THE ROOM DECORATED AND THIS HALF WILL GIVE US A SUPER DAY AT THE ZOO!

HOW KIND, DENNIS!

DAILY RASP

BOY AND DOG CATCH CROOK

FISH POND

WILL GNASHER CATCH THAT FLY? SEE LATER IN THE BOOK.

AT THE SEASIDE—

THESE NEWFOUNDLAND DOGS ARE SUPER! THEY'RE POWERFUL SWIMMERS AND FAMED FOR SEA-RESCUE.

I'M GOING TO TRAIN YOU TO BE A SEA-RESCUE DOG, GNASHER!

SO—

FETCH, GNASHER!

SCAMPER

GNA... BR...

BAH! YOU'RE HOPELESS!

MEANWHILE—

BLISSFUL SNOOZE

WOW! POOR OLD DAD'S DRIFTING OUT TO SEA!

COO! GNASHER'S GONE TO THE RESCUE!

GNASH

HO-HO! DAD'S STILL SNOOZING!

SWOOSH!

BANG!

WHAT HAPPENED?

GNASHER SAVED YOU, DAD—AND HE NEVER EVEN GOT HIS PAWS—

SHARP ROCK

BANG!

—WET?

TIME for TEASERS

1

GRR! MUTTER! SNORT! GROUSE! GRUMP! PEST! SNARL! GROAN!

Here are some of the CROSS words Dad uses when he hears of Dennis's latest piece of menacing. See if you can fit them into the puzzle.
We've given you the first word to start you off.

2

Dennis and Gnasher have hidden several of Dad's slippers. See how many you can find in this picture.

3

By moving one peashooter make a sum whose answer is 130.

4 NAPOLEON "BONE" APART A.

B.

C.

WISHING WELL D.

HA! HA! HO! HO! HEE! HEE! HEE! E.

TRY TO GUESS WHAT KIND OF BONES THESE PICTURES PORTRAY. THE FIRST ANSWER IS GIVEN.

5 Dennis wants to avoid taking a bath. Try and lead him to safety through the maze.

SAFETY

6 Can you identify Pie-face's pie collection?

A.

B.

C.

D.

GET TO SCHOOL!

RELUCTANT

IN A NEARBY PHONE-BOOTH—

THIS IS THE SCHOOL DOCTOR SPEAKING. I'M SENDING DENNIS HOME. HE MUST BE TREATED GENTLY AND HAVE ALL SORTS OF DELICACIES, AND HE MUSTN'T BE UPSET.

BACK HOME—

IT WORKED A TREAT! ROGER THE DODGER WOULD BE PROUD OF ME! CHOMP! CHOW!

SLEEPY

LOVELY!

SLURP!

SWOOSH!

THANKS FOR THE WATER, DAD!

NEXT DAY—

BUS STOP

DOCTOR, I'M WORRIED ABOUT DENNIS!

AND SO YOU SHOULD BE—ABOUT HIS CONDUCT—BUT NOT ABOUT HIS HEALTH—IT'S PERFECT!

MORE FLY CAPERS

GNASHER

GNASHER MUST CATCH THIS FLY SOON! SEE LATER IN THE BOOK.

NOW TO LOOK FOR SOMEBODY TO PING! AH, HERE COMES WALTER!

BUT—

HM! BET I COULD GET A BIRD TO TAKE THE CUP!

I'M ON MY WAY TO THE CAGE BIRD SHOW, AND I'M GOING TO WIN THE SILVER CUP!

LOVE BIRDS

I MUST GET JOEY THE BUDGIE SMARTENED UP, AND WIN THE CUP!

T JOEY'S MOULTING—

SQUAWK! GET LOST, DENNIS!

BAH! WE WON'T TAKE THE CUP WITH THAT SCRAGGY SPECIMEN!

I'LL GO BACK AND PING SOMEBODY WITH MY PEA-SHOOTER!

THEN—

ZOO

SNATCH

ERK!

OI! GIVE ME BACK MY PEA-SHOOTER, YOU OVERGROWN BUDGIE!

MUNCH!

DENNIS GETS THE PEAS BACK—

WOW! WHERE'S MY BIRD-DOG? GET HIM, GNASHER!

GNASH!

SQUAWK!

SNARL! GNASH!

GNASH!

SCREECH!

ZOO

HEAD IT TOWARDS THE BIRD SHOW, GNASHER!

THE CAGE-BIRD OW—

HERE'S A LATE ENTRY, FOLKS—NUMBER NINETY-TWO—OSWALD, SHOWN BY DENNIS THE MENACE!

JUDGE

23   24

THEN—

DENNIS'S BIRD HAS TAKEN THE CUP!

I TOLD YOU HE WOULD, WALTER!

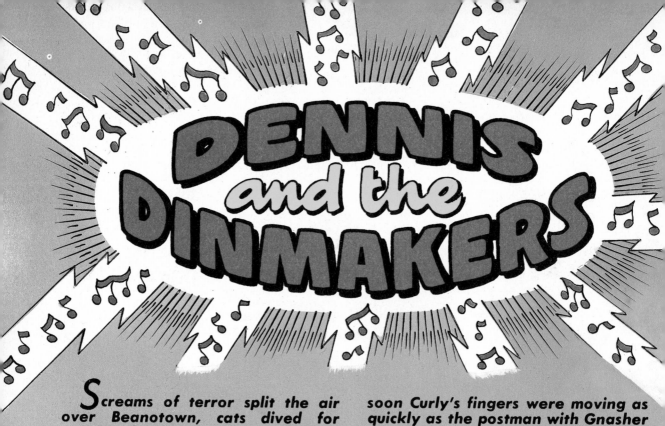

DENNIS and the DINMAKERS

Screams of terror split the air over Beanotown, cats dived for vacant dustbins, people suddenly decided to visit relatives—in Timbuctoo . . . You've guessed it—"Dennis and the Dinmakers" were about to have a band practice!

"I've been perfecting my fast guitar solo!" said Curly proudly. He'd only recently taken up the instrument. He used to play the penny-whistle until Dennis needed it to replace the pea-shooter that his Dad confiscated.

"Let's see!" asked Dennis and soon Curly's fingers were moving as quickly as the postman with Gnasher on his tail.

"OW! YAH! AARGH! YOWL!" screamed Curly. No, he wasn't singing–he had played so fast that his fingers had become entangled in his guitar strings and were now as twisted as his famous hair.

"Looks like we'll have to find a new group member," said Dennis sadly as Curly headed off to find a Boy Scout to untie the knots his fingers had developed. "What about Walter?"

" *That soppy Softy?*" hooted Pie-face crustily (he had his teeth in a pie crust at the time). " *Give me one good reason why we should ask him!*"

" *His Dad has a garage we can practise in,*" mentioned Dennis.

" *Let's ask him right away!*" agreed Pie-face.

They found Walter dressed in a suit of armour with a net in his hand.

" *Why are you wearing that, soft boy?*" asked Dennis.

" *I'm butterfly collecting and you never know when I might be buzzed by an angry Cabbage White!*" trembled the weedy lad.

" *We want you to join 'The Dinmakers'—can you play the guitar?*"

" *Horrors, no!*" squeaked Walter. " *I only play posh instruments like the grand piano, the violin and the cello!*"

" *You can't play the guitar? Excellent!*" smiled Dennis. " *You should fit into our group perfectly—we're not called 'The Dinmakers' for nothing!*"

A slight setback awaited the quartet as they entered Walter's Dad's garage—the new family saloon was in residence.

"**Never mind**," quoth Dennis, releasing the handbrake, "**soon get this out of here!**"

Unfortunately, Walter's drive happened to be on a slope.

"**Squeal!**" went Walter. "**Daddykin's car's running away!**"

"**Don't worry! It'll soon stop,**" said Dennis confidently.

SPLOOSH!

"**There—I knew your ornamental pond would stop its progress,**" grinned Dennis.

"**Right, pals!**" ordered Dennis, "**Let's play my latest composition, ' I call you my little turtle dove—you've**

They found just who they were looking for in an unusual place—Dad's compost heap. Yes, it was Rasher, Dennis's pet porker.

"**Let's try Rasher on mouth-organ!**" suggested Pie-face. But this proved a failure when Rasher swallowed the instrument whole and proceeded to make strange humming sounds every time he oinked.

Gnasher then had the bright idea of hanging tambourines on Rasher's tusks.

"**Good thinking, Gnasher!**" chuckled Pie-face. "**But how will we get Rasher to shake them?**"

COMPOST HEAP

got a big beak and pigeon toes '!"

Suddenly Dennis went a deathly white (which is very difficult to see when your face is in need of a wash). The reason for his pallor was the sweet strains of Hackingcoff's Ninth Symphony—Walter had tucked his guitar under his chin and was playing his favourite classical piece, using a bow Dennis had brought along to fire sucker arrows at passing Softies.

The Menaces immediately decided that Walter wasn't the right man for the job and left in search of a replacement for their replacement.

"Easy!" grinned Dennis, and, turning to the porker, he asked—

"How would you like a nice, hot, soapy bath, Rasher?" At that, Rasher shook his head so furiously that the tambourines rattled so loudly that rattlesnakes in a nearby zoo went green with envy.

It looked like the Dinmakers quest was over, but no—suddenly Rasher's nose twitched and—ZOOM!— off he rushed, giving a new meaning to the phrase "streaky bacon"!

"On, no!" groaned Dennis. "I forgot this was the day the swill lorry passed—that's our tambourine player gone, I'm afraid!"

Just then a wizened old figure appeared over the horizon. It was Dennis's Granny.

"Like to hear our pop-group?" asked Dennis to his ancient relative.

"Just a minute till I fetch my ear trumpet," came the reply.

"Hey! Why don't you play that in our group, Gran?" suggested Dennis eagerly.

Sadly, this again did not prove a success. As Granny let go a blast on her ear trumpet, small white missiles flew everywhere, breaking windows, knocking off policemen's helmets and giving rude awakenings to several cats...

PARP!

... Granny had forgotten she had a mouthful of her favourite peppermints.

As an angry crowd closed in on the old lady she decided that her career as a rock star was over.

"Let's practise in the park," suggested Dennis once the dust had settled, but on arrival their progress was halted by a rather officious parkkeeper who informed them gruffly—

"No dogs allowed except on a lead!"

Reluctantly Dennis attached a length of leather to Gnasher's collar.

"Never mind, old pal," consoled Dennis, "we'll make you our LEAD singer!"

" Who will play drums then?" asked Pie-face.

Just then a furious figure stormed up—Dennis's Dad had just been informed about Walter's Dad's car's involuntary dip.

" Ah, Dad!" simpered Dennis, *" I've just been telling Pie-face what a magnificent musician you are!"*

" You have?" gasped Dad, obviously taken aback. *" Well, I did play drums in the Boys' Brigade band, fifty—er—I mean, a year or two ago!"*

BA-DOOM-DUM-BAM!

Soon Dad was beating out a rhythm on the drums, but not with drumsticks—just look what the newest member of " The Dinmakers " is using—can you beat that?"

THE END

JUMP TO IT

GEOGRAPHY CLASS—

I FEEL ON TOP OF THE WORLD!

CLAP

CLAP

CEASE THIS TOMFOOLERY! THE LESSON IS ABOUT TO BEGIN!

PROD

YELPSH!

SUDDEN STOP

YES, AUSTRALIA IS ON THE OPPOSIT SIDE OF THE WORLD FROM BRITAIN

FASCINA

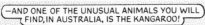

—AND ONE OF THE UNUSUAL ANIMALS YOU WILL FIND, IN AUSTRALIA, IS THE KANGAROO!

KANGAROO

TONIGHT, FOR HOMEWORK, YOU WILL DO AN ESSAY ON AUSTRALIA!

BACK HOME—

IF AUSTRALIA'S UNDERNEATH US, I SHOULD B ABLE TO DIG RIGHT THROUGH AND SEE ALL TH KANGAROOS AND THINGS.

LATER—

BAH! THIS IS HOPELESS! I'LL NEVER GET TO AUSTRALIA AT THIS RATE! LET'S GO FOR A DRINK OF LEMONADE!

GNASH!

THEN—

HAS ANYONE SEEN AN ESCAPED KANGAROO?

CIRCUS

HOP

HOP

OK, GNASHER! IF WE DON'T GET TO AUSTRALIA IN ANOTHER TEN MINUTES WE'LL GIVE UP!

GN

SUDDENLY—

CORKS! A K-KANGAROO! WE'VE DONE IT, GNASHER.

GNASHOO!

HOP

HOP

NEXT DAY AT SCHOOL—

—AND SO I DUG A HOLE RIGHT DOWN TO AUSTRALIA AND A KANGAROO JUMPED OUT AND HOPPED AWAY.

DENNIS'S ESSAY

QUIET PRIDE

VERY GOOD, DENNIS! YOU USE YOUR IMAGINATION!

BUT, TEACHER NOT IMAGINAT IT'S THE TRU

SNEEZY

HOI! STOP PLAYING WITH THESE DUCKS GNASHER!

SUCH FUN!

QUACK!

STOP RUNNING THROUGH ALL THOSE PUDDLES, GNASHER, YOU'LL CATCH A TERRIBLE COLD!

SOON—

GNASHOO!

WHAT DID I TELL YOU?

COME BACK AND BE PLASTERED!

WHAT ARE YOU TWO DOING? GLOOP!

SPLAT!

TRIP

YOU JUST CAN'T TREAT YOUR DAD LIKE THAT!

B-BUT, DAD, I WAS TRYING TO PUT IT ON GNASHER'S CHEST TO HELP HIS COLD!

AAA-AAA

STILL MORE FLY CAPERS

DON'T THINK GNASHER CAN TAKE MUCH MORE! SEE LATER IN THE BOOK.

TV TEE-HEE!

RATTLING

CUP TIE TODAY! ROVERS v RANGERS

COO! I MUST GO AND SUPPORT THE ROVERS!

THEN—

SIMPER! I'M GOING TO SUPPORT THE RANGERS!

CLICK! CLACK!

PAH! THAT'S TOO GOOD A RATTLE FOR A SOFTY LIKE YOU, WALTER!

THIS BABY'S RATTLE IS MORE YOUR STYLE!

RATTLE!

BUT—

WHIZZ!

CLANG!

SORRY, DENNIS! I DIDN'T REALISE IT WAS YOUR RATTLE!

THE MATCH WILL BE STARTING SOON— WHAT CAN I DO?

BRIGHT IDEA

EVEN MORE FLY CAPERS

GOOD FUN

RETURN THOSE RATTLES AT ONCE!

SO— I'LL MAKE MY OWN RATTLE.

TIN-CAN

RATTLE! CLATTER!

SWEET SHOP

AT THE MATCH—

RATTLE! CLATTER! CLACK! CLICK!

SOUNDS AS IF DENNIS GOT A RATTLE, READERS!

CLICK! CLICK! RATTLE! CLATTER!

I BOUGHT GNASHER AN ICE-LOLLY—NOW HE MAKES A SUPER RATTLE! UP THE ROVERS!

WHAT A "CAT"ASTROPHE

CRAZY CAMPING

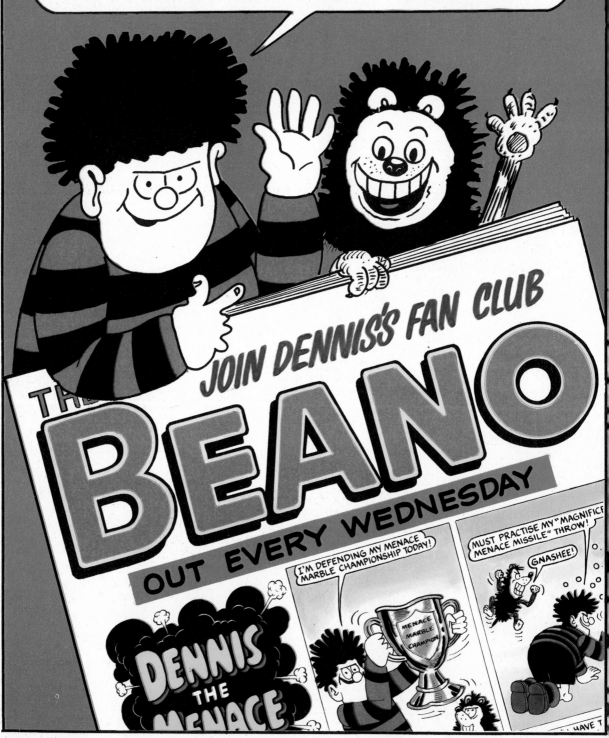

"YOU KNOW WHO" at the ZOO

GAME FOR

I'M TAKING MY UNCLE'S RETRIEVER, FLUSH, TO THE FIELD TRIALS THIS AFTERNOON. HE HAS TO SWIM ACROSS A LAKE AND RETRIEVE A STUFFED DUCK!

SOUNDS DELIGHTFUL! GNASHER AND I ARE OFF FOR A DIP AT THE BATHS, THEN WE MIGHT GO FOR A SPOT OF FISHING.

BUT AT THE BATHS—

NO DOGS ALLOWED!

PAY HERE

PUBLIC BATHS

BUT GNASHER'S JUST LIKE ONE OF THE FAMILY!

MEANWHILE—

BAH! MY LINE'S TANGLED IN THOSE REEDS! GO IN AND CLEAR IT, GNASHER!

SO—

HM! SOMEBODY'S LOST A STUFFED DUCK. I'D BETTER TAKE IT BACK WITH ME.

THIS PIKE SWAM UNDER MY NOSE, SO I JUST GRABBED IT, TOO!

WELL DONE, GNASHER! THAT'S A GOOD HAUL!

SPORTS SCENE

③

HIGH JUMP

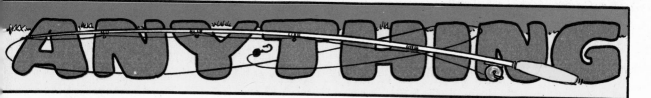

ANYTHING

THEY GO FISHING INSTEAD—
MOVE THAT WRETCHED MONGREL FROM OUR PATH!

CHEEK!

GAME FAIR
ANGLING CONTEST AND
GUN DOG TRIALS

GUN DOG TRIALS

NEXT!

FETCH IT, FLUSH!

BUT—

BRRR! THAT WATER'S TOO COLD!

EASILY THE FASTEST TIME OF THE DAY! YOUR RETRIEVER WINS THE CUP, LAD!

HOW NICE!

PLEASE ACCEPT THIS CUP FOR THE BIGGEST FISH LANDED TODAY!

GAME FAIR
ANGLING CONTEST AND
GUN DOG TRIALS

ENVIOUS

FLUSHED

OH, BOY! TWO CUPS! WHAT A DOG GNASHER IS!

ORCHARD KEEP OUT

PLUCK!
PLUCK

HIGH JUMP

HAR! HAR!

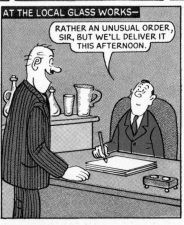

THE SHORT PAW OF THE LAW

EXCHANGE

...COULD HAVE DONE ...TH A LITTLE MORE ...LT.

ACTUALLY, THAT'S QUITE A GOOD IDEA OF DENNIS'S. IF WE HAD A 'PHONE, I COULD 'PHONE FROM THE OFFICE TO SAY IF I'D BE LATE.

LATER, AT TELEPHONE HOUSE—

I'D LIKE A RED ONE!

I'D LIKE A BLUE ONE!

I'D LIKE A WHITE ONE— SO THAT SETTLES IT— WE'LL HAVE A WHITE ONE.

ER-HELLO! WE'VE CHANGED OUR MINDS—WE'D LIKE A GREEN 'PHONE INSTALLED INSTEAD!

LATER—

GOOD! THAT COLOUR OF 'PHONE SUITS EVERYBODY!

NOT INTERESTED

A GREAT XYLOPHONE, TOO!

AND A VICE!

I'VE HAD ENOUGH OF THIS!

OUCH! GNASHER'S TEETH CAN ALSO BITE!

THROB! THROB!

ON GUARD!

Say it with

JUST the JOB

Hello,

DOLLIES!

A STICK-Y SITUATION

HEY, DAD! CAN I HAVE A PET?

BUT YOU'VE GOT GNASHER!

GNASHER'S NOT A PET— GNASHER'S MY PAL!

HISSSS! PAT PAT

HOW ABOUT A BABY BOA-CONSTRICTOR?

NOT LIKELY! THINK WHAT WOULD HAPPEN WHEN IT GREW UP!

WHY DON'T YOU STUDY THE SUBJECT OF INSECTS?

INSECTS, EH? I'VE JUST SPOTTED ONE— WALTER'S COMING DOWN THE ROAD!

STUDY OF INSECTS

HOW DO YOU LIKE MY STICK INSECTS, DENNIS?

YOU'RE HAVING ME ON! THAT'S ONLY A JAR OF OLD TWIGS!

TAKE A CLOSER LOOK!

CORKS! RIGHT ENOUGH! I'LL SWOP YOU THIS SUPER BOOK FOR THE WHOLE JARFUL!

WHERE CAN I KEEP MY NEW PETS?

WHAT AN INTERESTING BOOK!

LATER—

TIME I GAVE MY POTTED TREE A PRUNE.

SUDDENLY—

SCREECH!

SHRIEK! GET RID OF THOSE CREEPY-CRAWLIES!

STEADY ON, MUM! YOU'RE SCARING MY DEAR LITTLE PETS!

THEY'VE GOT TO GO, DENNIS!

SO—

DENNIS & CO STICK INSECT DEALERS BRANCHES EVERYWHERE 1 'BEANO' PER INSECT.

TA, DENNIS!

TRAINING SESSION

IN MANY BIG CITIES THEY HAVE UNDERGROUND RAILWAYS!

HOW INTERESTING!

DID YOU HEAR THAT, WALTER — OR CAN'T YOU HEAR TOO WELL WITH THAT PELLET BLOCKING YOUR EAR?

PING — PLUNK!

LATER —

I'D LIKE TO BE AN ENGINE-DRIVER WHEN I GROW UP!

BACK HOME — I'D BETTER START PRACTISING TO BE AN ENGINE-DRIVER!

DENNIS'S TOY BOX DAD, KEEP OUT!

SOON —

COME AND SEE MY UNDERGROUND RAILWAY IN THE LIVING ROOM, DAD!

HO! HO! BUT YOU CAN'T HAVE AN UNDERGROUND RAILWAY IN THE LIVING ROOM, SILLY BOY!

GULP — OR CAN HE?

RRR! SNARL!

HM! I DON'T THINK DAD REALISES HOW CLEVER I'VE BEEN!

I HOPE THE "TWO-FIFTEEN" IS ON TIME!

GOOD! IT'S BANG ON TIME!

RATTLE! CLICK!

HOWL!

TRIP

AT THE STATION —

I WANT TWO ONE-WAY TICKETS FOR AS FAR AS ONE NEW PENNY WILL TAKE US!

TICKET OFFICE

SNOW USE

YIPPEE! LET'S GET OUT AND PLAY IN THAT BEAUTIFUL SNOW, GNASHER!

BUT— HALT! CLEAR THE PATH BEFORE YOU PLAY!

SPLAT!

SLAM!

CRUNCH

GET BUSY, DENNIS. THAT'LL KEEP YOU OUT OF MISCHIEF!

GNASHERK!

FLUMPH!

HM! THAT TABLE GIVES ME AN IDEA!

THIS TABLE MAKES A SUPER SNOW PLOUGH!

BUT— BAH! WHAT A FEEBLE TABLE!

THEN— THAT LAWN-MOWER WOULD MAKE A GOOD SNOW-CLEARER.

THIS'LL BE GREAT FOR THE SNOW.

YIPPEE! NOW TO MOW THE SNOW!

GNASHOO!

BUT— DENNIS! DIG ME OUT OF HERE, AND, WHEN YOU'VE DONE THAT, I'VE GOT AN UNPLEASANT SURPRISE FOR YOU!

...ER...IT'LL TAKE SOME TIME, DAD...A LONG TIME!

TOP of the PUPS

WHAT A CARD

THE "BEANO" CAMERAMAN TRYING TO PHOTOGRAPH DENNIS'S DAD!

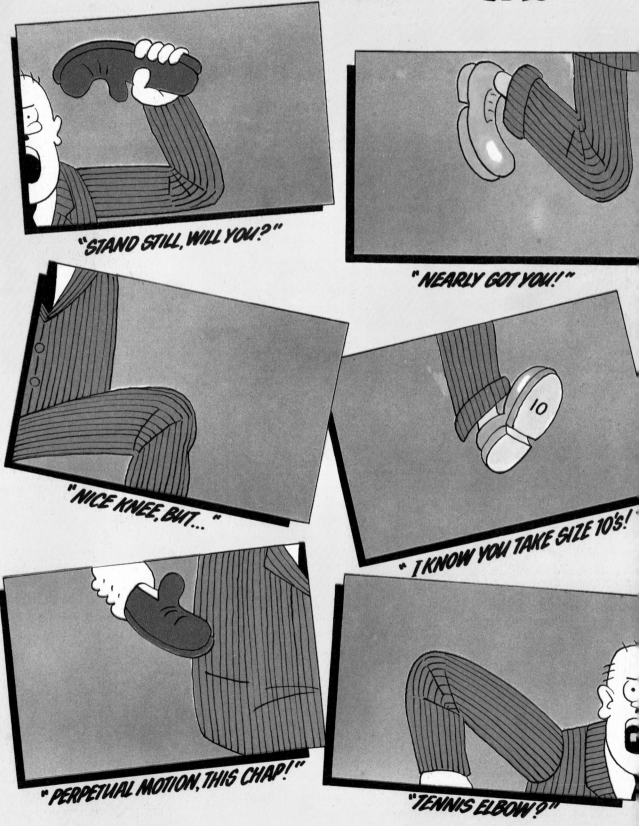

VICTORIA & ALBERT MUSEUM

Shawls

A STUDY
IN INDO-EUROPEAN INFLUENCES

By JOHN IRWIN

LONDON
HER MAJESTY'S STATIONERY OFFICE
1955

OTHER TITLES IN THE SAME SERIES

FRONTISPIECE. Fragment of shawl-cloth; loom-woven, Kashmir, eighteenth century. *See catalogue*

FOREWORD

THE history of shawls is inseparable from the larger subject of Indo-European artistic influences, and its treatment demands an understanding of both the Indian and European backgrounds. This monograph by Mr John Irwin, Assistant Keeper of the Indian Section, is based upon the Museum's large and important collection of shawls, divided between the Indian Section and the Department of Textiles; it is the first time they have been brought together for a single study.

LEIGH ASHTON
Director

iii

ACKNOWLEDGEMENTS

IN the preparation of this work I have frequently consulted colleagues in other museums and libraries, and for their generous co-operation in all matters relating to the supply of material and information my grateful thanks are due. In particular, I would like to acknowledge the help given by Mr W. G. Archer, Keeper of the Indian Section, Victoria and Albert Museum; Miss Gira Sarabhai, of the Calico Museum of Textiles, Ahmedabad; Miss Gertrude Townsend, Keeper of Textiles, Museum of Fine Arts, Boston; Mr C. H. Rock, Director of Paisley Museum; Mrs R. Barker, Keeper of Art, Castle Museum, Norwich; Miss Anne Buck, Curator of the Gallery of English Costume, Manchester; and Mr C. S. Minto, City Librarian and Curator, Edinburgh; and Mrs A. C. Weibel, of the Detroit Institute of Arts. In problems relating to weaving technique, I have consulted Mr J. F. Flanagan, formerly of the Royal College of Art, whose experience in this field is perhaps unrivalled.

I am also indebted to the Countess of Powis, Mr W. McIntyre, Mr R. Cruickshank and Mrs M. MacCormack for permission to include among the plates shawls from their private collections.

JOHN IRWIN

June, 1954

CONTENTS

v

SHAWLS

I. THE KASHMIR SHAWL

IN adopting the Kashmir shawl, Europe took to herself something more than a new style of garment. She assimilated a new conception of textile design which was to stimulate and enlarge the scope of her decorative tradition.

Design formerly had been conceived on the flat, even when intended for costume. But Kashmir shawls were seen at their best when hanging in folds, with their curved motives off-set by the poise of the human body. Although European designers had been slow to grasp this idea, once assimilated it came to influence a very large field. In fact, the world has not yet tired of the Kashmir cone which, under the name 'Paisley pattern', is as conspicuous a feature of *popular* textile design today as it was of *exclusive* fashion a hundred and fifty years ago.

Although the main debt is on the European side, the story of the Kashmir shawl is a reminder that such influences are seldom unreciprocal. Europe's borrowings from India have always been counterpoised by India's simultaneous borrowings from Europe. Even more significant is the fact that borrowings on either side were usually drawn, not from what was fundamentally indigenous in the other culture, but from precisely those features which were eclectic in the first place. A striking example of this is provided by Indo-European textile history of the seventeenth century. Many Restoration crewel-hangings to the Englishman are at once 'oriental' in style; but to an eye disciplined in Indian tradition, this debt would appear slight. The reason is that the chintz designs which inspired the crewel-work hangings would seem from the *oriental* standpoint to be themselves mainly European—a reminder that they were designed for foreign taste in the first place. Similarly, a lady of Victorian England who valued her Kashmir shawl for what she supposed to be its authentic Indian quality, would have been shocked to know that the Kashmiri who designed it had in all probability been working with a French pattern-book at his elbow.

These are among the facts which arise from the study of shawl-history, giving it a broader interest and significance than it might at first be expected to offer.

ORIGIN AND TECHNIQUE

The Persian word *shāl*, from which the English 'shawl' is derived, originally denoted a class of woven fabric rather than a particular article of dress. In traditional usage, *shāl* could equally well apply to a scarf, a turban, a mantle, or even a coverlet, the distinguishing feature being that the material was fine wool or some other kind of animal fleece. The Italian traveller Pietro della Valle, writing in 1623, observed that whereas in Persia the *scial* or shawl was worn as a girdle, in India it was more usually carried 'across the shoulders'.[1] This fact, confirmed by contemporary portraits, gives India some claim to be regarded as the true home of the decorative shawl, in the sense in which it became known in Europe: a loose enveloping shoulder-mantle woven, either partly or wholly, in animal fleece.[2]

Worn in this way in India, the shawl was essentially a male garment; its degree of fineness was traditionally accepted as a mark of nobility. Although a garment so simple in shape and form undoubtedly has a long history in the Near East,[3] the finest shawls of the modern era are synonymous with the name of Kashmir.

The origins of the industry in Kashmir are obscure. According to local legend, recorded more than a hundred years ago,[4] the founder was Zain-ul-'Abidīn (A.D. 1420–70), whom historians have called the Akbar of Kashmir, in recognition of his enlightened rule and promotion of public works. Zain-ul-'Abidīn was said to have introduced Turkistan weavers for the purpose. Although unproved, this suggestion is of some significance, for when we come to accounts of the industry in the early nineteenth century we find that one feature distinguishing it from traditional weaving in India proper is the technique employed. This technique has parallels in Persia and Central Asia but nowhere on the Indian sub-continent as far as evidence is available. Western textile historians have called it the twill-tapestry technique, because of its similarity in some respects to the technique traditionally employed in Europe for tapestry weaving. According to this, the wefts of the patterned part of the fabric are inserted by means of wooden spools (Kashmiri, *tojli*) without the use of a shuttle. Weft threads alone form the pattern; these do not run the full width of the cloth, being woven back and forth round the warp threads only where each particular colour is needed. In other respects, the Kashmir technique differs from tapestry weaving, the loom being horizontal instead of vertical, and its operation more like brocading.

---

[1] Pietro della Valle, II, p. 248.

[2] This definition applies for the purposes of this study. Shawls made *entirely* of silk, cotton or materials other than wool are therefore excluded.

[3] Heredotus, in the fifth century B.C., described Egyptians as wearing a woollen garment in terms which indicate a shawl (Book II, 81).

[4] Baron Charles Hügel, p. 118.

Applied to shawls, the twill-tapestry technique was slow and laborious and demanded a high degree of specialization. The traditional practice was for the patterned section of a shawl to be produced on a single loom (the field, if plain, being woven separately on a simple loom with shuttle). In the case of a rich design, this meant that a shawl might take eighteen months or more to complete. In the early nineteenth century, however, when designs became more elaborate and trading methods more competitive, a new practice was introduced of dividing the work of a single shawl among two or more looms. In this way, a design which had formerly occupied one loom for eighteen months could now be produced by two looms in nine months, or by three looms in correspondingly less, and so on. After the various parts of a design had been separately woven, they were handed over to the needleworker (*rafugar*) who joined them together, the joins being executed with such subtlety and fineness that it is often impossible to detect them with a naked eye. In 1821, Moorcroft described this method of distributing work among several looms as a recent introduction.[1] He mentioned as many as eight looms being engaged on a single shawl; but later in the century this number was often exceeded, and there was one report of a shawl being assembled from 1,500 separate pieces.[2] These are sometimes called 'patchwork shawls'.

Another important innovation introduced at the beginning of the nineteenth century was the *amli* or needleworked shawl, which was ornamented entirely with the needle on a plain woven ground. (It must be added, however, that even the *tilikar* or loom-woven shawls often betray *some* signs of needlework, because a *rafugar* or embroiderer was usually responsible for the final touching-up of the loom-woven pattern. This touching-up sometimes included the reinforcing of colours where needed, and occasionally even more fundamental modifications to the design.) The type of shawl with an *entirely* needleworked pattern, however, was unknown in Kashmir before the nineteenth century. It was introduced at the instigation of an Armenian named Khwāja Yūsuf, who had been sent to Kashmir in 1803 as the agent of a Constantinople trading firm. It had not previously occurred to merchants that simulation of the loom-woven patterns by the much simpler process of needle-embroidery on a plain ground required very much less time and skill, and consequently less outlay. The ingenious Khwāja Yūsuf saw his chance, and with the help of a seamster by the name of 'Ali Bābā

---

[1] MSS. Eur. D.260.

[2] Colonel J. A. Grant, quoted in *Kashmeer and its shawls* (Anonymous), p. 48.

produced the first needle-worked imitations for the market at one-third of the cost of the loom-woven shawls.[1] Besides this enormous saving in production costs, the needleworked shawls at first escaped the Government duty levied on the loom-woven shawls, which in 1823 amounted to 26 per cent of the value. As a result, enormous profits were made, and this branch of the industry expanded rapidly. In 1803 there were only a few *rafugars* or embroiderers available with the necessary skill for the work. Twenty years later, there were estimated to be five thousand, many of them having been drawn from the ranks of former landholders,[1] dispossessed of their property by Ranjit Singh in 1819, when Kashmir was invaded and annexed to the Sikh kingdom.

A cloth intended to serve as the ground of an *'amli* or embroidered shawl was first placed on a plank and rubbed with a piece of highly-polished agate or cornelian, until perfectly smooth. After this, the design was transferred from paper to the cloth by pouncing with coloured powder or charcoal. For the needlework, stem-stitch and satin-stitch were most commonly used; and in order to make the stitches as flat as possible against the ground (and therefore similar to the woven patterns), care was taken to nip up individual threads of the warp in the stitching. Moorcroft described the needlework of the first *'amli* shawls as being less perfect and having the raised or embossed appearance of traditional Indian chain-stitch work, the improved method being learned subsequently from embroiderers of Kirman province in Persia.[2] Needleworked shawls were made throughout the nineteenth century, and apart from those simulating loom-woven patterns, many were made with scenes depicting human figures, which will be discussed later in the section devoted to style. It is important to add here, however, that after about 1850 there was a marked deterioration in the technique of many *'amli* shawls—particularly those with human figures—and some of the embroiderers resorted to a comparatively coarse chain-stitch, sometimes executed on a cotton ground.[3]

The material traditionally used for Kashmir shawl weaving was fleece derived from a Central Asian species of the mountain goat, *Capra hircus*. This was popularly known in the West either as *pashmīna* (from Persian *pashm*, meaning in fact any kind of wool) or *cashmere*, from the old spelling of Kashmir. The latter term is particularly misleading, because all shawl-wool used in Kashmir

---

[1] Moorcroft, MSS. Eur. 113, pp. 33 ff.

[2] MSS. Eur. D.260, p. 4. See also MSS. Eur. E.113, and D.264.

[3] The fact of the matter is that late *'amli* shawls are very variable in quality. A possible explanation is that the coarser kinds were made in the Punjab by less skilled hands.

was imported from Tibet or Central Asia in the first place and was not at any time produced locally.[1]

The fleece was grown by the animals as a natural protection against the severities of the winter climate of those regions. It appeared beneath the rough outer hair—the finest being derived from the under-belly—and was shed on the approach of summer. Although goats were the main producers of shawl-wool, a similar fleece was derived from wild Himalayan mountain sheep such as the Shapo (*Ovis orientalis vignei*), the Argali (*Ovis ammon*), the Bharal (*Pseudois nayaur*), and the Himalayan Ibex (*Capra ibex*).[2] It was even claimed that Tibetan shepherds' dogs sometimes grew the same fleece.[3]

Most of the fleece reaching Kashmir belonged to one of two distinct grades. The best and most renowned for its soft silkiness and warmth was known as *asli tūs*, which was derived only from the *wild* animals, collected from rocks and shrubs against which the animals rubbed themselves on the approach of warm weather. The extreme fineness of this grade was probably due to the greater heights at which the animals wintered, and it was this material which gave rise to well-known stories of shawls being so fine that they could be drawn through a thumb-ring—the so-called 'ring-shawls' of Mughal fame.[4] However, the number of shawls woven in pure *asli tūs* was probably never more than a very small proportion of the total, owing to its comparative scarcity, the higher import duties charged upon it, and the much greater time and effort required for its cleaning and spinning. In 1821, the annual imports of *asli tūs* were said to constitute less than one-sixth of the total bulk of other shawl-wool imports, and in the whole of Kashmir there were only two looms specializing exclusively in the weaving of pure *asli tūs*.[5]

The second grade of shawl-wool was derived from domesticated goats of the same species, and this provided the bulk of the raw material for Kashmir looms. Prior to 1800, most of it came from Ladakh and Western Tibet. Shortly after the turn of the century, however, there was an epidemic among goats in these areas,

---

[1] To add to the confusion over the use of the term *cashmere*, the British textile trade has now adopted a new definition unrelated to the raw material. According to the Director of the Shirley Institute, Manchester, the term is used 'to describe a certain type of cloth *formerly* woven from yarns spun from goat fibres', and he includes cloth woven with any high-quality wool yarn. 'The weave must be 2/1 weft twill with a larger number of picks than ends per inch, giving what is also known as the "cashmere twill" or "plain back" weave.' (From a letter to the author dated 19.3.1954.)

[2] Moorcroft, MSS. Eur. E.113.

[3] G. T. Vigne, II, 124, and C. E. Bates, p. 55.

[4] Manucci, II, p. 341.

[5] Moorcroft, MSS. Eur. D.260, pp. 1-2.

and henceforth supplies were derived mainly from herds kept by nomadic Kirghiz tribes and imported through Yarkand and Khotan. In the second half of the century the main source was Sinkiang, and in particular Turfan.[1] As supplies at this period were seldom enough to meet demand, goat-fleece became increasingly expensive in relation to other wools. This encouraged adulteration and a general falling off in traditional standards, which was undoubtedly one of the factors contributing to the decline of the shawl trade in the 1860s, to be discussed later.

ORGANIZATION OF THE INDUSTRY

The earliest detailed account of the Kashmir shawl industry is that written by William Moorcroft between 1820 and 1823, preserved in manuscript at the Library of the old India Office (now the Commonwealth Relations Office), Whitehall, London. These reveal a situation in which division of labour was far advanced, to the extent of twelve or more independent specialists being involved in the making of a single shawl.

First among these were the spinners, who were women working in their own homes. The raw material was given to them in a very dirty condition, their first task being to separate it into fine fleece, inferior fleece, and hair. The fine fleece constituted only about one-third of the total weight, and this had to be further divided into two grades of fineness, the second being known as *phīri* or seconds wool, which was reserved for inferior shawls. The yarns were spun into lengths of about 2,500 yards, then doubled and twisted, and for this work the spinners earned a maximum of about one and a half annas or three-halfpence a day.[2]

The dyers constituted another separate group, buying and selling yarn independently. Moorcroft quotes them as saying that in Mughal times more than three hundred tints were in regular use;[3] but by the beginning of the nineteenth century when he was writing, this number had been reduced to sixty-four. Most of these were vegetable dyes: blues and purples from indigo; orange and yellow from carthamus and saffron; reds mainly from logwood. But other sources were also used, including cochineal for crimson, and iron filings for black. Oddly enough, green was said to have been extracted from imported English baizes or broadcloths, which were boiled for the purpose.[4]

---

[1] Baden Powell, pp. 43 ff.
[2] Moorcroft, MSS. Eur. E.113, p. 7.
[3] *Ibid.*, Eur. F.38, letter dated 21.5.1820.
[4] Vigne, II, p. 127; and Moorcroft, MSS. Eur. E.113, p. 10.

1. Abdullah Qutb-Shāh of Golconda wearing a Kashmir shawl.
Painted about 1670   *British Museum, Add. Mss.* 5254

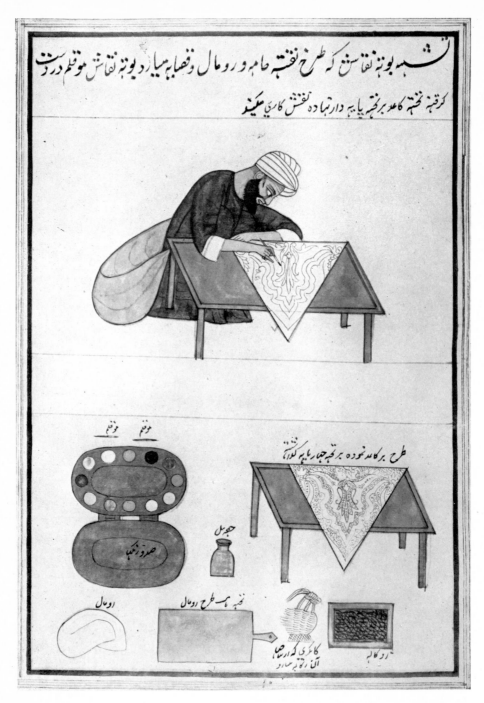

2. The pattern-drawer (*naqqāsh*) and his implements. Painted by a native artist, *c.* 1823   *India Office Library, Oriental vol.* 71

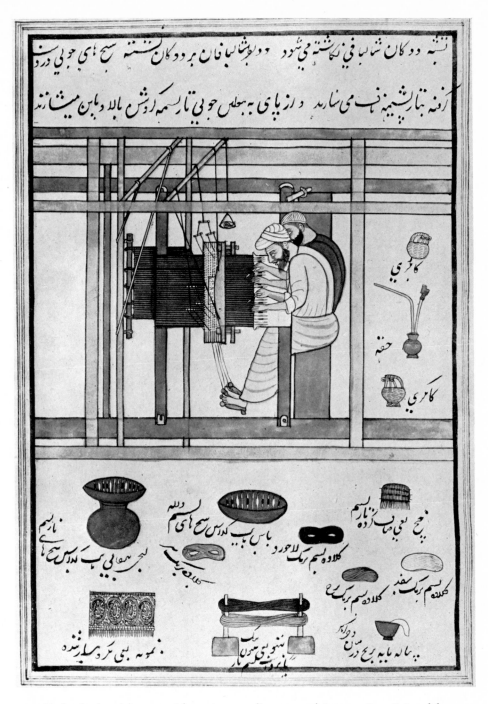

3. Kashmir shawl-loom, with various appliances used in weaving. Painted by a native artist, *c.* 1823   *India Office Library, Oriental vol.* 71

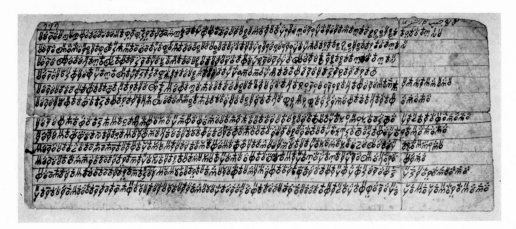

4. *Ta'līm* or coded pattern-guide, as used by Kashmir shawl-weavers.
Acquired in Kashmir in 1881   *Victoria and Albert Museum, I.M.33–1924*

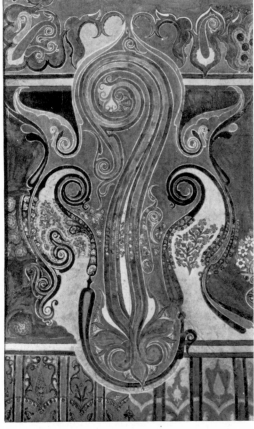

5. Designs from a shawl-weaver's pattern-book. Acquired in Kashmir in
1881   *Victoria and Albert Museum, I.M.32–1924*

Before weaving could begin, at least six other specialists were involved. These were the warp-maker, warp-dresser, warp-threader, pattern-drawer, colour-caller and pattern-master.

It was the warp-maker's job to twist the yarn into the required thickness for the warp (usually 2,000 to 3,000 double-threaded warps being required for a shawl); the warp-dresser's to starch the warps, and the warp-threader's to pass the yarns through the heddles of the loom.

The importance of the pattern-drawer, or *naqqāsh* (*see* Illus. No. 2), is indicated by the fact that he received the highest pay—far higher even than that of the weaver.[1] Pattern-drawers were few in number, and in the second half of the century, when the industry was very much expanded, the art was still said to be confined to only five or six families.[2] The pattern-drawer sometimes coloured his own drawing (Illus. No. 5), but usually choice and disposition of colour were left to the colour-caller (*tarah gurū*). With a black-and-white drawing before him, the colour-caller, beginning at the bottom and working upwards, called out each colour, the number of warps along which it was required to extend, and so on, until the whole pattern or section of pattern had been covered. This was taken down by the pattern-master (*ta'līm gurū*) and transcribed into a kind of shorthand intelligible to the weaver. An original transcription or *ta'līm* is shown at Illus. No. 4, and in the painting reproduced at Illus. No. 3 the weavers can be seen working with one before them.

Besides those who prepared the warps of the main part of the shawl, an entirely separate group of specialists prepared the silk warps of the narrow outer borders or edgings. The use of silk warps for these parts was intended to give them more body or stiffness so that the shawl would hang better. However, this had the disadvantage of causing uneven shrinkage and sometimes spoiling the shape of a shawl when washed.

The weavers were all men, foremost among whom were the *ustāds* who owned the looms. The cost of a shawl-loom in the early nineteenth century varied from one and a half to five rupees (approximately 3s. to 10s.), and a *ustād* might own anything from three to three hundred looms, each normally employing three operators.[3]

There were two main systems of contract between the *ustād* and those who

---

[1] According to Moorcroft, pattern-drawers earned from 2 to 8 annas a day according to skill, compared with the weaver's maximum of 1 anna a day. He calculated 1 anna as being equal to one penny.

[2] C. E. Bates, p. 56.

[3] Only two operators when a very simple pattern was involved.

7

worked his looms. One was based on piecework, whereby the weavers received a fixed sum for every hundred spools passed round as many warps (allowing a maximum earning in Moorcroft's time of about one anna or a penny a day per man, increasing to about double this sum in 1870).[1] A second system was based on partnership, whereby the loom-owner advanced the loom and raw materials and took one-fifth of the net proceeds of sale.

The spools or *tojlis* with which the weavers worked in place of shuttles were made of light, smooth wood and had both ends charred to prevent their becoming rough or jagged in use. Each spool held about three grains of yarn; and the number used in the weaving of a pattern varied from 400 to 1,500, according to degree of elaboration. In the process of weaving, a cloth was faced downwards and the weaver inserted his spools from the reverse side. After each line of weft had been completed to his satisfaction, the comb was brought down 'with a vigour and repetition of stroke which appear disproportionately great to the delicacy of the materials.'[2] One of the ways by which merchants determined the quality or standard of weaving was by counting the number of comb-strokes or wefts to the *girah* (one-sixteenth of a yard).

In 1821, Moorcroft wrote that there were 'sometimes as many as fifty looms in a single house, though more commonly not half this number.'[3] Later in the century, however, a hundred or more looms were sometimes concentrated together. 'I went to inspect one of the largest manufactures in Kashmir,' wrote a traveller in the 1860s. 'The proprietor, a Mohammedan, employs 300 hands. His house is a handsome, three-storied building, well aired and lighted, and the workers are seated at their looms like clerks at their desks . . .'[4]

Moorcroft described the main profit-makers of the industry not as the loom-owners but as the *mohkuns* or shawl-brokers, who were intermediaries between the producers and foreign merchants. Later, as the result of the concentration of loom-ownership into fewer hands, there arose a new class in the form of owners of large manufactures, known as *kārkhānādārs*. The term *uatād* was then applied to those who worked as foremen or supervisors for the *kārkhānādār*.[5]

The weavers were the most oppressed section of the industry, the majority being depicted as ill-clothed, under-nourished, and permanently in debt.

[1] C. E. Bates, p. 54.

[2] Moorcroft, MSS. Eur. E.113, p. 17.

[3] *Ibid.*, p. 16.

[4] Colonel Grant, quoted in *Kashmeer and its shawls* (Anonymous), p. 48.

[5] C. E. Bates, p. 53.

Moorcroft wrote that without the supplementary earnings of wife and children the average weaver could not even support a family.

After Kashmir had been handed over by the British to the Maharaja Gulab Singh in 1846, conditions for the weavers deteriorated even further. The Maharaja levied a poll-tax of Rs. 47–8 per annum on each shawl-weaver;[1] and in order to ensure a constant income from this source he introduced a law forbidding any weaver—whether half blind or otherwise incapacitated—to relinquish his loom without finding a substitute (a condition almost impossible to fulfil). On top of this, an *ad valorem* duty of 25 per cent was charged on each shawl, and its assessment and collection was farmed out to a corrupt body of officials, whose own illegal exactions were said to have amounted to a further 25 per cent of the value.[2]

In face of such oppression, hundreds of weavers adopted the dangerous course of fleeing the country—an escape made difficult by the limited number of mountain passes and the fact that they were guarded. As a measure of the despair which drove weavers to this course, it must be remembered that it involved deserting their families and the knowledge that they would be victimized as hostages.[3]

Those who successfully escaped settled in Punjab towns such as Lahore, Amritsar, Ludhiana, Nurpur, Gurdaspur, Sialkot, Gujarat, Kangra and Simla, all of which produced their own 'Kashmir' shawls. Shawl weaving had been established at Lahore (probably by Kashmiri immigrants) at least as early as Akbar's reign (A.D. 1556–1605),[4] and in the mid-seventeenth century the French traveller Bernier also mentioned Agra and Patna in this connection. He added that the shawls woven in these cities were inferior in softness and texture to genuine *kashmirs*, which he attributed to the poorer quality of the water of the plains.[5] A more likely reason was the difficulty of obtaining the best goat-fleece. For centuries Kashmir had monopolized the main sources of supply, and owing to the lack of suitable passes linking Central Asia with the plains of Northern India it was difficult to divert supplies.[6] As a result, shawl-weavers working in the plains were often compelled to adulterate goat-fleece with Kirman sheep's wool.[7]

---

[1] A reduction of Rs. 11 was made in 1867.
[2] C. E. Bates, pp. 54–7, and R. Thorp, *passim*.
[3] R. Thorp, p. 36.
[4] *Āīn-i-Akbarī*, I, 32. See also *Pelsaert*, p. 36, and *Manrique*, I, p. 429.
[5] Bernier, p. 402.
[6] Torrens, p. 93
[7] Baden Powell, p. 43.

The earliest documentary references to the Kashmir shawl industry appear in literature of Akbar's reign (A.D. 1556–1605), but unfortunately they throw no light on style. In the *Aīn-i-Akbarī*, or Institutes of Akbar, the Emperor is revealed as a keen admirer of the shawls who not only kept his wardrobe well stocked with them but introduced the fashion of wearing them in pairs (*doshāla*), stitched back-to-back, so that the undersides were never visible.[1] From the same source we learn that *kashmirs* were already at this period renowned as gifts and sent to distant countries.[2]

There are indications that the shawls most coveted during the early Mughal period were embellished with gold and silver thread. In 1630, Manrique described the finest examples as having 'borders ornamented with fringes of gold, silver and silk thread. They [the Princes and Nobles] wear them like cloaks, either muffling themselves up in them or else carrying them under their arms. These choice cloths are of white colour when they leave the loom, but are afterwards dyed any hue desired and are ornamented with various coloured flowers and other kinds of decoration, which make them very gay and showy.'[3] Shawls of this type are often mentioned in the early records of the English East India Company as being useful articles of bribery. Sometimes they were offered by native officials to the Europeans, and Sir Thomas Roe, James I's ambassador to the Mughal court, records in characteristic language how he indignantly rejected such a bribe offered by the Governor of Surat soon after his arrival in 1616: 'And pressing me to take a Gold Shalh, I answered we were but newly friends: when I saw any constancy in his carriage and the money paid, I would be more free with him, yet I would receive no obligation . . .'[4]

In 1866, Bernier wrote that shawls measured about 5 ft. by 2½ ft. and had plain fields, decoration being limited to the end-borders or heads, which were *less than one foot in depth*.[5] This shallowness of the end-borders appears to have been characteristic until the beginning of the nineteenth century when, as will be shown, they were suddenly enlarged. Thévenot, Bernier's contemporary,

---

[1] *Aīn-i-Akbarī*, II, 15.

[2] *Ibid.*, I, 32.

[3] Manrique, I, 428–9. These of course bear no relation to the comparatively coarse shawl-goods embroidered with gold thread 'in the Kashmir style', and produced in large quantities in the Punjab in the late nineteenth century.

[4] Roe, p. 223.

[5] Bernier, p. 403.

mentions that the ground colour varied, but that Hindus favoured follimort or dead-leaf (*de feuille-morte*).[1]

The earliest surviving shawl-piece in a public collection is a fragment preserved in the Calico Museum of Textiles, Ahmedabad (Plate 1). It consists of part of an end-border with a repeat of delicate, freely-spaced flowering plants, rendered in the semi-naturalistic style of the late seventeenth century. Shawls with similar end-borders are often depicted in portraits of the Golconda school of painting, a typical example being the portrait of Qutb-Shāh at Illus. No. 1, facing p. 6.

At this period the characteristic motive of Kashmir shawl-design was a slender flowering plant with roots (Fig. 1). It combined the grace and delicacy of Persian floral ornament (from which it was ultimately derived) with the naturalism characteristic of seventeenth-century Mughal art. In the early eighteenth century, this simple floral motive was treated more formally, and the number of flowers stemming from a single plant increased (Fig. 2). At about the same time it ceased

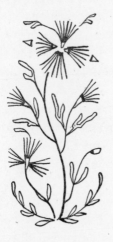

FIG. 1. *c.* 1680   FIG. 2. 1700–1730

to be depicted as a flower with roots and merged with another well-known Indo-Persian decorative motive—the conventional vase-of-flowers. Many of the eighteenth-century forms betray their dual origin by retaining both the vase and the appearance of root-growth. The name given to these floral motives was *būṭā*, meaning literally 'flower', and it was not until the middle of the eighteenth

---

[1] Thévenot, III, p. 37.

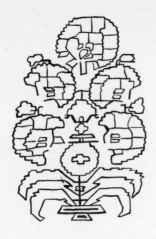
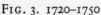

FIG. 3. 1720–1750   FIG. 4. 1740–1770

century that the outline of the motive began to harden into the rigid formal shape which later came to be known in the West as the *cone* or *pine* (but still known in Kashmir as *būṭā*). Although this motive had antecedents in Near Eastern textile patterns of the seventh or eighth centuries A.D.,[1] the cone in the varied forms in which it became associated with shawls was clearly the product of separate development.

Independently of the Kashmir *būṭā*, another type of cone based on the leaf-form appeared more or less simultaneously in Persian decorative art. This Persian form had an important influence on the subsequent development of the Kashmir cone, giving rise to a variety of cone forms which were common to Indo-Persian art of the period.

A further stage was reached in the first quarter of the nineteenth century, when the Kashmir cone began to lose trace of its naturalistic, floral origin and became a purely conventional form (Fig. 6). This prepared the way for a final stage of abstraction when the cone became elongated and transformed into a scroll-like unit as part of a complicated over-all pattern (Fig. 8).

As guides to dating, the different stages in the development of the cone must be regarded with caution. Because a certain form came into vogue at a certain period, it did not necessarily follow that earlier types were superseded. In fact, it often happened that the older well-tried motives and patterns outlived the new.

Kashmir shawls were first worn in fashionable circles in the West in the third quarter of the eighteenth century, and by 1800 the shawl trade between Kashmir

---

[1] O. Falke, fig. 35; and A. C. Weibel, fig. 51.

12

FIG. 5. 1770–1800

FIG. 6. 1815 onwards

and the West was well established. The appearance of European agents in Kashmir added fresh colour to an already cosmopolitan scene. 'At this city,' wrote Moorcroft from the capital, Srinagar, in 1822, 'I find merchants from Gela and from other cities of Chinese Turkestan, from Uzbek, Tartary, from Kabul, from Persia, from Turkey, and from the provinces of British India engaged in purchasing and in waiting for the getting up of shawl goods differing as to quality and pattern *in conformity to the taste of the markets for which they are intended* in a degree probably not suspected in Europe.'[1] Some indication of the diversity of

FIG. 7. 1820–1830

FIG. 8. 1850–1870

---

[1] Moorcroft, MSS. Eur. G.28, letter dated 12th November, 1822.

tastes for which the Kashmiri weaver catered is indicated by the descriptions of shawl-goods given in Appendix II, compiled by Moorcroft during his three-year investigation into the shawl industry. In the preparation of designs for the Western market, one merchant in particular—an Armenian named Khwāja Yūsuf (already mentioned as the originator of the 'amli or needleworked shawl, p. 3)— appears to have had an important influence. He had been sent to Kashmir in 1803 by a trading firm at Constantinople, in order to have shawls made according to patterns that he took with him.[1]

Khwāja Yūsuf's original idea in introducing the needleworked shawl was to simulate and undersell the loom-woven patterns. About 1830, however, the needleworkers began producing a distinct style of design with human figures, usually illustrating one of the well-known poetical romances of Indo-Persian literature, such as the *Khamsa* ('Five Poems') of Nizami (*see* Plate 23), and the *'Iyār-i-dānish* ('Criterion of Knowledge') of Abu'l Fazl. It was said that Ranjit Singh (who held dominion over Kashmir from 1819 to 1839) especially admired this type of shawl and advanced five thousand rupees for a pair to be worked with scenes illustrating his victories (only one of which was completed).[2] Later in the century, 'amli shawls were sometimes embroidered in the form of a map of the capital, Srinagar.[3]

The nineteenth-century popularity of the Kashmir shawl in Europe undoubtedly owed much to romantic associations with the 'mysterious and unchanging East'. The new popular journalism of the period was always ready to foster such associations, and this led to the publication of innumerable articles by unqualified authorities setting out to explain the alleged antiquity of Kashmir motives and patterns and even ascribing to them an elaborate symbolism. Typical of them is an article which appeared in the magazine *Household Words*, founded by Charles Dickens: 'If an article of dress could be immutable, it would be the [Kashmir] shawl; designed for eternity in the unchanging East; copied from patterns which are the heirlooms of caste; and woven by fatalists, to be worn by adorers of the ancient garment, who resent the idea of the smallest change . . .'[4] Repetition of such nonsense over a long period had its effect. On the one hand, it belied the true character of the Kashmir industry as a living and developing

---

[1] Tessier, p. 27.

[2] Vigne, p. 124.

[3] A map-shawl, embroidered in 1870, was published in the *Magazine of Art*, London, vol. 25, 1901, pp. 452–3.

[4] *Household Words*, 28th August, 1852.

tradition adaptable to changing conditions; and on the other, it obscured the important influence exercised upon those changes by European taste.

One way of tracing the development of Kashmir designs in the nineteenth century is by examining shawls depicted in contemporary European portrait painting and costume engravings. These show that the shawl most popular in the first two decades was of rectangular shape with a plain field and large semi-naturalistic floral cones in the borders.[1] Examples are often depicted in French portraits of the period, particularly in the works of Ingres whose portrait of Mme Rivière, painted in 1805, is reproduced at Illus. No. 6, facing p. 26. Similar shawls feature in his portraits of Mme la Comtesse de Touron (1812), Mme de Senonnes (1814), Baronne Popenheim (1818), and the Stamaty Family (1818).[2]

A distinctive feature of the cone at this period was its streamer-like bending tip, reminiscent of the earlier cypress-and-almond-tree motive of Persian art.[3] By 1815, the semi-naturalistic floral cone had begun to give way to a more formal, abstract type (Figs. 6 and 7). Shawls with a diapered or trellised field were also coming into favour, and among these was the square shawl with a medallion in the centre and quarter medallions at each corner, known as the *chand-dār* or 'moon shawl' (Plate 14). In 1823, Moorcroft remarked that Persian taste favoured shawls in which the pattern 'almost completely covers and conceals the colour of the ground'; and this probably refers to shawls of the type shown at Plates 20 and 21.

The mid-nineteenth century was a period of great prosperity for the merchants and dealers, and also one of artistic decline, when foreign taste increasingly dominated shawl design. The French were the main instigators, and it was in the year 1850 that the first French agents arrived in Kashmir with a mission to 'improve' the traditional designs.[4] In the following decade, many visitors to Kashmir reported—sometimes with approval but more often with alarm—that 'French patterns and new colours, such as magenta, are beginning to prevail over the genuine Indian designs.'[5] One of these accounts is perhaps worth quoting in full:

'The great estimation in which Cashmere shawls are held in France, and the

---

[1] The French shawl merchant Rey, writing in 1823, stated that prior to this period the cone was never more than nine inches in height. J. Rey, p. 146.

[2] Most of these are reproduced by H. Lapauze, *Ingres, sa vie et son oeuvre*, Paris, 1911.

[3] Textile historians usually refer to this motive as the cypress 'bent by the wind'; but in fact it represents the natural form of the tree, the topmost shoot of which always bends.

[4] B. H. Baden Powell, p. 41.

[5] Colonel J. A. Grant, quoted in *Kashmeer and its shawls* (Anonymous), p. 48.

consequent demand for them, have induced some of the large houses in that country to keep agents in Srinugger [Srinagar, capital of Kashmir]. One result of this is that the French design patterns in Paris and send them out to Cashmere for execution. Although these designs are all in the oriental style, they are no improvement upon the old work of the natives . . . "The French patterns," says Mr Simpson, who brought to the country an experienced artistic eye, "were perhaps purer than the old; they contained more free and sweeping lines, but they wanted the mediaeval richness of the native taste. It may be described as the difference between a piece of Rococo ornament and what an artist of the thirteenth century would have produced. There was a distinguishing character about the original style which is being rubbed out by this foreign influence".[1]

From other accounts we learn that the weavers themselves resented this foreign interference. 'At first (and in fact until within a few years) much difficulty was experienced in persuading the native designers to alter or amend their patterns. They were attached to their old style and would not accept alteration; but now this difficulty has been overcome and the weavers are willing to adopt hints, in fact they now seldom begin to work till the pattern has been inspected or approved by the agent for whom they work.'[2]

Although Simpson's explanation of the French contribution to Kashmir design is not very clear in expression or terminology, it nevertheless gives important clues. In referring to the 'mediaeval richness' of the traditional as opposed to the French patterns he probably had in mind the marginal ornament of mediaeval European illuminated manuscripts, before which the eye is made to wander restlessly, in convolutions, in marked contrast to what he calls the 'free and sweeping lines' of the French or 'rococo' style, so characteristic of the late designs of both Kashmir and European shawls.

European intervention in the preparation of designs was so general at this period that when Kashmir shawls were shown at the contemporary international exhibitions of 'art and manufactures', the European agent who commissioned a shawl was given full credit for the design. At the Exhibition of Punjab manu-factures held at Lahore in 1873, first prize was awarded to an Amritsar shawl designed by an Englishman, Mr R. Chapman.[3]

Sometimes, when a merchant was dissatisfied with a finished shawl, he cut out

---

[1] William Simpson, *India ancient and modern*, p. 5. Simpson, a well-known English water-colourist, visited Kashmir in 1860 to paint shawl weavers and embroiderers. Two of his paintings are reproduced in the above work.

[2] Letter from an Amritsar shawl agent, quoted by B. H. Baden Powell, p. 41.

[3] B. H. Baden Powell, p. 45. The particular shawl is reproduced in the forementioned work, facing p. 45.

certain sections of the pattern and ordered others to be substituted. In this way, the whole appearance of a shawl was sometimes changed while in the merchant's hands.[1]

In the 1860s Kashmir produced the reversible shawl, the pattern being identical on both sides of the cloth. This did not reflect any significant departure in technique, but was achieved by skilful trimming of the loose weft threads on the reverse side, and the outlining of all the main details in the pattern by needlework. The example at Plate 33 was shown at the Paris Exhibition of 1867 and bears its original exhibition label which reads: 'Scarf of quite a new fabric. Shows the same on both sides. Sent by Diwan Kirpa Ram,[2] Kashmir. Price: £37 12s 0d.'

From about the second quarter of the nineteenth century, Kashmir had to face competition from Persia;[3] but lacking the former's longer experience of patterned shawl-weaving, the Persians were never able to produce shawls of comparable quality. There were two types of Persian shawl which have to be mentioned. The first is woven in the same twill-tapestry technique, the patterns being influenced by those of Kashmir but at the same time distinguished by bolder floral treatment and a more architectural emphasis in design. Moreover, the predominant colour is a rather deep red not at all characteristic of Kashmir. A few specimens of this type survive in museum collections, usually in the form of coverlets or prayer-mats.[4]

The second type of Persian shawl which competed with Kashmir in the nineteenth century was known as the *Hussain Qūli Khān*. These are even more easily distinguishable by the fact that they were woven in silk on harness-looms, the unused sections of the wefts on the underside being left floating. In pattern, they are often copies of Kashmir fabrics, and the Victoria and Albert Museum possesses two pieces—a *Hussain Qūli Khān* and a Kashmir piece—which are identical in pattern.[5]

Besides woven imitations, Persia also produced embroidered shawls in the Kashmir style, an example being shown at Plate 36. (The fact that such shawls bear Persian inscriptions is not in itself an indication of Persian origin, because the Persian script was in common use in Kashmir.)

---

[1] B. H. Baden Powell, p. 46.

[2] This was the name of the Prime Minister of Kashmir at that time.

[3] Describing Kirman province, the French traveller Dubeux remarked '. . . on y voit un grand nombre de manufactures de châles qui imitent ceux du Caschmir.' *La Perse*, p. 57.

[4] Examples in the Victoria and Albert Museum (Textile Dept.) are T.41–1932, T.39–1912, 1061–75, 1061a–75, and 346–1880.

[5] Nos. 1064–1875 and 885–1877.

Between 1850 and 1860, shawl exports to Europe more than doubled, far exceeding the total estimated output of the whole industry at the beginning of the century.[1] In the following decade, however, there was a sudden contraction in the market. The average Kashmir shawl of that time (such as the example shown at Plate 52) was no longer equal to the best products of the Jacquard looms of Lyons and Paisley (Plates 48, 49 and 51), and yet were more expensive to buy. On top of this decline came the Franco-Prussian War of 1870–71, resulting in the closure of the French market for *kashmirs*, and the simultaneous and quite sudden eclipse of the shawl as an article of fashion. From being the pride of every girl at her marriage and coming-of-age, the shawl was relegated to the grandmother's wardrobe. As a result, the Kashmir industry, so long geared to Western demands, was doomed. Collapse of trade was followed by the severe famine of 1877–79, when shawl-weavers are said to have 'died like flies'. Most of the survivors, having hands so refined and delicately adjusted to the technique of shawl-weaving that they were useless for most other occupations, subsequently died in destitution.[2] Only the needle-workers experienced temporary respite, adapting themselves to the embroidering of coverlets, table-cloths and similar goods for the tourist market. Within a generation of its final phase of prosperity the shawl industry was dead, and the art of its weavers irrecoverably lost.

---

[1] The export figures were £171,000 in 1850–1, and £351,000 in 1860. Estimates of the earlier output are based on Moorcroft MSS. Eur. E.113, p. 29.

[2] According to evidence handed down verbally, some Kashmir shawl weavers were recruited for carpet-knotting.

2. THE SHAWL IN EUROPE

W<small>E</small> have seen how Western influences affected the shawl in Kashmir during the nineteenth century. We must now consider the development of the shawl in Europe.

There are references in the trade records of the East India Company to 'shawles', 'chales' and 'chawools' being shipped in bulk to England as early as the seventeenth century.[1] It can be shown, however, that these were not shawls in the later European sense but piece-good material or *shāl*-cloth, woven from goat-fleece in Kirman Province, Persia. These 'Carmania shawles' were much in demand among hatters of Restoration England for making imitation 'beavers', and also among women for petticoats.[2]

Perhaps the earliest reference to the shawl as a garment of fashion in Europe appears in one of Sterne's letters to Eliza, dated 1767. It would even be in keeping with Eliza's character to suggest that she herself may have started the fashion in London, by bringing a selection of *kashmirs* with her when she sailed from Bombay in 1765. Once introduced, the shawl rapidly gained in fashionable esteem, and by 1777 was well known as an article of dress in England.[3]

The main attraction of the *kashmir* at this period was its warmth and un-equalled softness of texture, which qualities were admired before colour or pattern. It was the former features too which appealed to British woollen manu-facturers; and knowing that prices up to 200 guineas were being paid for *kashmirs* in Britain, they were determined to produce a native cloth to stand comparison.

NORWICH

Credit for the first British shawls is usually given to Edward Barrow, of Norwich, who began the manufacture in 1784.[4] However, these were not shawls in the true sense, but a kind of cotton neckerchief of small dimensions em-broidered in imitation of the flowered muslin neckerchiefs of Bengal. Moreover, they were cheap products intended primarily for export to America.

---

[1] I. O. Archives, Letter Book VII, f. 40; *Home Miscellaneous*, vol. X, f. 119. See also *Birdwood*, pp. 27, 40 and 65.

[2] *Ibid.*, Letter Book VIII, f. 40; Fryer, p. 331.

[3] *Philosophical Transactions* (Royal Society), vol. 67, pt. 2, 1778, letter dated 17.4.1777.

[4] *General History of the County of Norfolk*, I, p. xciii; and Sir Frank Warner, pp. 290–1.

Nevertheless, Norwich must still be regarded as the pioneering centre of the imitation shawl industry in Europe. For this, the real credit is due to an enterprising manufacturer, John Harvey, who experimented throughout the 1780s with yarns derived from Spanish and Norfolk flockwools.[1] No description exists of Harvey's first shawls; but in 1791 another Norwich manufacturer, Philip James Knights, attracted publicity through being awarded a silver medal by the Society of Arts for a 'Shawl Counterpane', judged 'equal in beauty, and far superior in strength to the India counterpanes'.[2] The feature which most attracted attention was its size, being four yards square and woven in one piece. The pattern was needle-embroidered; the centre being left plain 'for the coat-of-arms of the family who may become the purchaser'.

There is no indication that the patterns embroidered on shawls of this period copied oriental designs. As will be shown presently, Edinburgh weavers were probably the first to imitate the *kashmir* in pattern as well as texture. The first Norwich shawls with Kashmir patterns did not appear until 1803, and these were produced entirely in the harness loom. There is no clear indication why this had not been attempted previously; but a possible reason is that no woollen yarn is likely to have been strong enough to bear the strain imposed on harness-loom warps. John Harvey overcame this difficulty by combining silk warps and woollen wefts, and although some writers have vaguely ascribed an earlier date for the use of this combination in shawls, there is no suggestion that it had previously been used in a harness loom. The *fillover* was the name given to this new type; so-called because 'in the weaving the face of the shawl is downwards, and all the work composing the figure is filled over it . . .'[3] This may be taken to mean that on the 'wrong' side details of the pattern were obscured or 'filled over' by floating wefts.

The earliest *fillover* patterns were probably simple repeats on a plain ground, but their success was immediate and established Norwich as the leading centre of British shawl weaving for the next twenty-five years. As *fillover* weavers became more practised, patterns were elaborated, and some fine examples of the 1830s are shown at Plates 37, 38 and 39.

In spite of their debt to Kashmir, the best of these designs are notable for originality in conception and treatment. Borrowed motives are imaginatively blended with those of English origin, while sensitive drawing unites the different elements and stamps the whole with harmony and individuality.

---

[1] *Transactions* (Society of Arts), vol. vii, 1789, pp. 167 ff.

[2] *Ibid.*, vol. x, 1792, pp. 196 ff.

[3] *Report from Assistant Hand-loom Weavers' Commissioners*, pt. 1, 1839, p. 318.

A surprising amount of capital was required in preparing the harness loom for a new *fillover* design. In some cases as much as £100 was spent before weaving even started, and this explains the importance of the so-called 'manufacturer', who provided the capital and commissioned the work, as distinct from the weavers who executed the work on their own looms at home.

Prices of good Norwich *fillovers* ranged from twelve to twenty guineas, but occasionally a specially commissioned piece cost as much as fifty.[1] When the Norwich *fillover* industry was at its most prosperous, in the 1820s and early 1830s, weavers sometimes earned very high pay: in one case a manufacturer claimed that he was paying a man and his wife £15 a week between them for *fillover* weaving.[2]

By the late 1830s, Norwich was beginning to suffer in competition with Paisley. The Scottish manufacturers were unscrupulous in pirating successful Norwich designs and undercutting them. Giving evidence before the Handloom Weavers' Commissioners in 1838, a leading Norwich manufacturer complained: 'The people of Paisley imitate our shawls, not less than four out of every six which we bring out. No sooner does one of our shawls, which we have designed and brought out at great expense, take with the public, but within six weeks or two months the market is inundated with Scotch goods of the same sort, and at prices which take away our profit.'[3] Relief from this situation came two years later, when the functions of the Patent Office were extended to include the registration and copyright protection of textile designs; but by this time Paisley had already established a commercial lead in the shawl trade. As will be shown, Paisley's success was due ultimately to more efficient organization and to greater division of labour, introduced at a time when Norwich manufacturers were content to depend upon a reputation already established. Typical in this respect was the tardiness with which Norwich adopted the revolutionary invention of the Jacquard loom. This greatly facilitated and cheapened pattern-weaving for the handloom weaver, as will be explained later. Whereas the Jacquard loom had been in general use at Paisley by 1845,[4] it was not used at Norwich for shawl-weaving until five years later, and then only for comparatively unambitious patterns with small repeats. The first Norwich shawl to be entirely woven on a Jacquard loom was shown at the 1851 Exhibition and subsequently bought by Queen Victoria.[5] Norwich continued shawl-weaving on a small scale until the

---

[1] *Report from Assistant Hand-loom Weavers' Commissioners*, I, 1839, p. 305.
[2] *Ibid*, I, 1839, p. 305.
[3] *Ibid*, pt. 1, 1838, p. 388. See also G. K. Blyth, p. 60.
[4] *Paisley Herald*, 12th November, 1859.
[5] Great Exhibition of 1851: *Illustrated Catalogue*, p. 326.

1860s, when the last of the big firms, Messrs Clabburn, Sons & Crisp, ceased this line of business.[1] Henceforth, Norwich became the main retailing centre in England of French shawls. The latter are sometimes mistaken for shawls of Norwich manufacture, on account of their commonly bearing the stamp of the Norwich retailer. For instance, all French shawls sold through the agency of the Norwich firm of Caley bore a stamp in gold letters which read as follows:

'Caley, Shawlman and Silk Mercer to the Queen and Princess of Wales, Norwich. Importers of Continental Manufacturers'.[2]

EDINBURGH

Although Norwich was the pioneer centre of British shawl weaving, the finest and most costly of all early imitation shawls came from Edinburgh. Unfortunately, there is little that can be said about Edinburgh shawls, because there are only few and short references in contemporary records. Moreover, only one shawl-piece known for certain to be of Edinburgh origin—and that of a comparatively late period—is traceable today.

However, particular interest attaches to the Edinburgh shawl, not only because it was the first to imitate the *kashmir* in style as well as in texture, but because the earliest examples were made by a brocading technique not far removed from the so-called twill-tapestry technique employed by weavers in Kashmir.

In the second half of the eighteenth century Edinburgh was an important centre of damask weaving. Shawls are first mentioned in 1792,[3] and, according to the evidence of an Edinburgh shawl merchant, John Wigham, who wrote the article on *shawls* in the seventh edition of the *Encyclopædia Britannica*, published in 1842, they were woven on damask looms. Wigham's firm, J. and J. Wigham, was one of the early firms to engage in the weaving of shawls in the Sciennes district of Edinburgh, which lends special weight to the evidence. It is also worth bearing in mind that the *Encyclopædia Britannica* was at that time published from Edinburgh and already jealous of its reputation for scholarly accuracy. In the same article it is implied that the brocaded shawls were not

---

[1] This firm often stamped its shawls: 'Messrs Clabburn, Sons, and Crisp, Shawl Manufacturer. Awarded Gold Medal, ... Exhibition.' It does not follow from this, of course, that each shawl bearing such a stamp was the actual specimen which won the award, although this has sometimes been supposed by shawl-owners concerned.

[2] A shawl bearing this stamp, and obviously of French origin, is preserved at the Victoria and Albert Museum: T.177–1929.

[3] *Statistical Account of Scotland*, 1793, vol. VI, p. 594. A later authority, Mr W. Cross, writing in 1872, stated that the founder of Edinburgh shawl weaving was a merchant named Kennedy, who was 'supplied by some of the nobility with specimen [Kashmir] shawls to copy'. W. Cross, p. 8.

made for long, as they were found too expensive, and that Edinburgh weavers subsequently adopted the harness loom. This must have been after 1803 when, as already explained, John Harvey, of Norwich, had for the first time made it possible to weave patterned shawls on the harness loom. It is not unreasonable to suppose that it was the introduction of the Norwich *fillover* that made the brocaded shawl of Edinburgh too expensive, which would make the year 1804 the date of the change-over.

Another interesting fact about the early Edinburgh shawl industry is that the spun silks used in the most expensive Edinburgh shawls were sent to Norwich for dyeing.[1] This points to a close connection between the two centres.

At the beginning of the century there were said to have been a thousand hands engaged in shawl-weaving at Edinburgh; but as a result of later competition from Paisley this number was gradually reduced, until by 1840 there were only about a hundred.[2] Seven years later, the last Edinburgh loom producing imitation shawls stopped work.[3] It belonged to the firm of David Sime & Son, and a sample fabric registered in the name of that firm, in the same year, is preserved at the Patent Office and reproduced here at Plate 44.

PAISLEY: THE FIRST STAGE, 1808–25

The Paisley shawl industry originated as an off-shoot from Edinburgh.

Situated a few miles to the south-west of Glasgow, Paisley had first come into prominence as a weaving centre in the second half of the eighteenth century, in competition with Spitalfields. As a result of the Spitalfields Act, which fixed a minimum scale of prices for London silk weavers, some manufacturers are said to have transferred capital to the North in order to take advantage of cheaper labour which towns such as Paisley could offer.[4] But by the beginning of the nineteenth century the demand for silk gauzes had fallen off, and Paisley weavers were ready to turn to another field of specialization.

The standard of living at Paisley was lower at this time than that of Edinburgh, and it seems probable that Edinburgh manufacturers commissioned shawls from

---

[1] 'When the best and most expensive shawls were made in Edinburgh, the manufacturers there were obliged (in consequence of superiority in colours) to send all the spun silk that they required to be dyed crimson and scarlet to Norwich, as no other place could furnish such colours on spun silk as they were obliged to use . . . ' (*Report from Assistant Hand-loom Weavers' Commissioners*, pt. I, 1839, p. 305).

[2] *Encyclopædia Britannica*, 7th edn., Edinburgh, 1842.

[3] *Paisley Herald*, 12th November, 1859. The records at the Patent Office show that Edinburgh went on producing plain and striped shawls, unrelated to Kashmir patterns, for some years.

[4] John Wilson, p. 243.

Paisley weavers for the same reason that silk manufacturers had earlier started them on silk gauzes.

The first step was taken soon after the turn of the century, when a number of Paisley weavers were induced by higher wages to move to Edinburgh to learn shawl weaving.[1] (It is tempting to conclude that this coincided with the period when Edinburgh manufacturers were abandoning the brocading technique for shawls and were needing outside experience in harness weaving.) A further stage was reached in 1808–9, when, instead of encouraging more Paisley weavers to move to Edinburgh, the same manufacturers decided to commission twelve of them to weave shawls in their own home town.[2] Once introduced into Paisley, shawl-weaving grew rapidly in importance, and within a few years it had become the main industry of the town.

In the early days of Paisley shawl-weaving there was little division of labour. The weaver prepared his own patterns and tied his own harnesses for the loom.[3] Designs were correspondingly simple. The first important advance was the introduction in 1812 of the 'ten-box lay',[4] which was a device allowing five shuttles to be held in the loom simultaneously, thus greatly facilitating the weaving of multi-coloured patterns. As a result, Paisley weavers were able to attempt *exact* reproductions of Kashmir patterns. Accordingly, enterprising manufacturers posted agents to London to take copies of the latest shawl designs as they arrived from India. Tracings were made and despatched at once to Paisley; and within another eight days imitations were leaving for the London market. These were priced at about £12, in competition with the originals at £70 or £100. So successful was this policy that by 1818 Paisley imitations had found markets in competition with true *kashmirs* as far afield as Persia and Turkey.[5] Thus encouraged, Paisley manufacturers attempted the Indian market itself. In the following year several consignments were despatched with this end in view, and in Moorcroft's letters written from India in 1820 and 1821 there are several accounts of how they were received: 'At first sight the Shawl Merchants of this country were deceived, but on handling them a look of surprise has spread over their countenances, and on closer examination they discovered that the shawls were not of Kashmeeree fabric. They gave great credit to British artists for their

---

[1] W. Cross, p. 8.

[2] *Paisley Herald*, 12th November, 1859.

[3] W. Cross, p. 8.

[4] *New Statistical Account of Scotland*, 1845, p. 271; and *Paisley Herald*, 12th November, 1859. Both sources state that the 'ten-box lay' was introduced from Manchester.

[5] *The Weavers' Magazine*, 20th October, 1818.

close imitations, but considered them as inferior to the Kashmeeree originals, and exhibited substantial reasons in support of their opinion. They showed with obvious gratification the superior softness, fullness and richness of feel of Kashmeeree over British shawl-cloth, of equal number of thicknesses of thread. This superiority, which must be admitted by a candid examiner, arises from the greater softness of the goat wool and from a looser twist in the Kashmeeree yarn . . .'[1]

At this period most Paisley shawls were woven either with silk or cotton warps and woollen or cotton wefts, or with silk yarn throughout. But as the texture of these shawls was still generally admitted to be inferior to the true *kashmir*, it was recognized that the only answer would be to obtain independent supplies of the authentic goat-fleece.

THE QUEST FOR TRUE SHAWL-WOOL

Direct trade with Tibet or Central Asia was not at that time a practical proposition. For centuries the very limited supplies of shawl-wool coming from that source had been monopolized by Kashmiri merchants, and in recent times this monopoly had been confirmed by treaty between Kashmir and Ladakh—the small principality bordering Western Tibet (now part of Kashmir) through which most of the supplies passed. Under pressure from British shawl manufacturers, the East India Company in 1819 commissioned George Rutherford, an officer in their service, to investigate possibilities of diverting supplies into British India; but these efforts met with little success. The few bales he managed to secure were shipped to England between 1821 and 1823, only for the manufacturers to discover that the precious fleece had become so thickly felted with coarse hairs in transit that it could not be economically separated.[2] The financial loss incurred as a result discouraged the Company from making further efforts in this direction.

Supplies from Tibet and Central Asia being impracticable, the alternative was to try naturalizing the shawl-goat in Britain. This had been thought of as early as 1774, when Warren Hastings (himself a keen admirer of Kashmir shawls, many of which he bought for his wife)[3] commissioned George Bogle to visit Tibet and to procure 'one or more pairs of the animal called *tūs*, which produce the shawl wool.'[4] At this stage neither Hastings nor Bogle was aware that the

---

[1] MSS. Eur. F.38, letter dated 21.5.1820. Moorcroft implied that Norwich as well as Paisley shawls were reaching India.

[2] *Transactions* (Society of Arts), vol. 46, 1828, p. 131.

[3] S. C. Grier, *passim*. A pair of gloves woven in Kashmiri shawl-cloth and formerly belonging to Hastings is preserved at the Indian Institute, Oxford.

[4] G. Bogle, p. 8.

animal they named after its wool (*tūs*) was in fact a goat. Nor apparently was the Teshu Lama of Tibet, for in response to Bogle's request he supplied only sheep.[1] In 1783, Hastings sent another mission to Tibet; this time knowing what nature of animal was concerned. Captain Samuel Turner, who led the expedition, procured a number of goats; but on bringing them down into the hot plains of Bengal the animals were at once afflicted with a 'cataneous eruptive humour' from which most of them died. The few survivors were shipped to England but arrived so sickly that they all 'very shortly after perished'.[2] Eight years later the idea of importing the goats was again revived, this time by the newly-founded Society for the Improvement of British Wool. Sir John Sinclair, its energetic president, wrote to everyone in a position of influence whom he thought might help, including such unlikely individuals as Sir William Jones, the eminent Sanskrit scholar.[3] However, Sinclair's perseverence eventually brought results. In 1793, the Directors of the East India Company notified him that their agents at Bussora, in Persia, had procured 'two animals that produce the shawl-wool.'[4] They arrived in England the same year and were sent first to the private zoo at Earl's Court, London, owned by John Hunter, the famous surgeon.[5] It was intended that Hunter should make some crossing experiments before forwarding them to Sinclair in Scotland, but this plan was frustrated by the early death of the female without progeny. Nothing more is heard of the male, except that it was exhibited to the delight of the crowds at the carnival of St Bartholomew at Smithfield, under the description of 'a savage beast . . . snared on the lofty and barbarous mountains of Thibet.'[6]

It is a coincidence that about this time William Moorcroft, who has been extensively quoted in the first chapter in connection with his investigations into the Kashmir shawl industry between 1820 and 1823, arrived in London from the north of England, a young man of twenty-four, to seek Hunter's advice about his career. Having had already some medical training at an infirmary, Hunter advised him to specialize as a veterinary surgeon.[7] Moorcroft followed Hunter's advice,

---

[1] *Philosophical Transactions* (of the Royal Society), vol. 67, pt. 2. 1778, letter dated 17th April, 1777.

[2] Samuel Turner, pp. 356–7.

[3] Jones replied that he was much too busy to help, being 'engaged from morning to night in arranging the new digest of Indian laws.' *Life, writings and correspondence*, p. 208.

[4] These were almost certainly local Kirman goats, not the authentic shawl-goat. Kirman goats had provided fleece for the 'shawles' sent to England in the seventeenth century (see p. 19); and in the 1670s unsuccessful attempts had been made to establish a colony of these goats on the island of St. Helena (India Office Archives, Letter Book V, *passim*).

[5] T. Baird, p. 25.

[6] J. Foot, p. 10.

[7] H. H. Wilson, p. xx.

6. Portrait of Mme Rivière, by Ingres. Painted in 1805
Musée du Louvre, Paris

7. English Jacquard loom, *c.* 1870.   From J. Murphy, *History of weaving*

and it was in this capacity that he was sent to India by the East India Company. Whether or not he had actually seen the shawl-goats in Hunter's zoo, there is no doubt that from an early stage he had nursed the ambition of successfully naturalizing them in Britain. Encouragement, both official and non-official, was never lacking. In 1808 (the year Moorcroft left for India) there appeared in a publication of the Board of Agriculture the colourful statement that successful naturalization of the shawl-goat 'would offer a richer prize to our manufacturers than the acquisition of the golden fleece.'[1]

In 1812, Moorcroft got permission to lead an expedition into Western Tibet and returned with fifty shawl-goats.[2] On being embarked for England, however, the male animals were segregated on one ship and the females on another. This proved a blunder, for the ship carrying the females was wrecked with total loss on the way home. Of the lonely male goats which arrived in the other ship, the majority were sick and dying, and only four survived the last stage of the journey to Blair, in Scotland, where they were to be kept on the estate of the Duke of Atholl. Within a few months even these died, and once again the experiment ended in total failure.[3]

The next and most ambitious attempt of all was made under French auspices. M. Guillaume Louis Ternaux, a well-known shawl manufacturer, obtained the semi-official support of the French Government to sponsor an expedition to Tibet to acquire a flock of goats. The expedition was led by M. Amédée Joubert, a Turkish language professor at the Bibliothèque Royale, who was already well known as a traveller.[4] Joubert left France in 1818 and travelled first to Turkey, then Russia. On reaching Astrakhan, he was told that there was no need to go to Tibet, because goats of similar species were kept by Kirghiz tribes on the steppes of Western Kazakhstan. Satisfied with the evidence produced for him, he bought 1,289 animals and turned for home. By the time he reached France most of the goats had died; the rest suffered severely from a scab disease similar to that which had afflicted shawl-goats in Britain. However, between two and three hundred recovered sufficiently to be made the subject of experiments. Of these, two pairs were bought by an Englishman, Mr Tower, for separate trials in Essex.[5] Initial results on both sides of the Channel were disappointing. The yield

---

[1] R. Bakewell, pp. 108–9.

[2] *Asiatic Researches* (Asiatic Society of Bengal), vol. xii, 1816.

[3] *Brande's Journal*, vol. 9, p. 330; *Quarterly Review*, July 1820, and *Calcutta Government Gazette*, 10th May, 1821.

[4] Tessier, p. 25.

[5] *Transactions* (Society of Arts), vol. 46, 1828, p. 130.

of fleece was extremely low, the male goats averaging about 4 ozs. per year, and the females only half this amount. At this rate, there was little prospect of home supply ever becoming an economic proposition, although, on the grounds of quality alone, there was some satisfaction. In 1828, when Mr Tower's original flock had increased to twenty-seven, sufficient fleece was obtained for three shawls. These were subsequently woven by Messrs Millar & Sons, of Paisley, and were widely admired, one of them being awarded a Gold Medal by the Society of Arts.[1]

Meanwhile, experiments were being made in France by crossing the Russian species with Angora goats. This increased by five times the quantity of fleece produced,[2] and although unable to fulfil more than a very small fraction of the demands of French industry, these goats continued to be a source of shawl-wool for some years.

Joubert's expedition was the last serious attempt to naturalize the shawl-goat in Europe. But the idea was never entirely dropped, and in 1846, when the British Government made over Kashmir as an independent state to the Maharaja Gulab Singh and his heirs, the transfer was conditional upon an annual tribute of 'one horse, twelve perfect shawl-goats of approved breed (six males and six females), and three pairs of Cashmere shawls.'[3] The tribute of goats was later commuted for a small money payment; but the tribute of shawls continued throughout Queen Victoria's reign (it was said that she bestowed them upon her ladies-in-waiting) and was rescinded on the accession of Edward VII.

To the indefatigable Moorcroft, obsessed with the idea of making British shawls supreme over all competitors, it was not enough to be defeated in attempts to naturalize the shawl-goat. With the same zeal he embarked upon a campaign to naturalize (or at least to promote the immigration of) whole families of Kashmiri spinners, weavers and pattern-drawers. The idea was that they should be settled at Paisley and Norwich ('on very light terms of remuneration') in order to instruct those engaged in the imitation shawl trade. As this campaign never bore fruit, and therefore had no influence upon shawl history, it would not be relevant to discuss the details here. But as the story includes much of interest to the student of the period, excerpts have been included in Appendix II.

PAISLEY: THE SECOND STAGE, 1825–40

Finding it extremely difficult to obtain supplies of the authentic shawl-wool,

---

[1] *Transactions* (Society of Arts), vol. 46, 1828, p. 131.
[2] *Ibid*, vol. 49, 1833, p. 49.
[3] Article X of the Treaty of 16th March, 1846.

Paisley manufacturers again directed their attention to producing substitutes. From the many references to 'Thibet shawls' being woven at Paisley in the 1820s and 1830s, it might be thought (in common with public opinion at the time) that these were all woven in the coveted goat-fleece. It is worth recalling in this connection a passage in the Epilogue of Scott's novel *The Surgeon's Daughter*, published in 1827:

> She made a digression to the imitation shawls now made at Paisley, out of real Thibet wool, not to be known from the actual country shawl, except by some inimitable cross-stitch in the border. 'It is well,' said the old lady, wrapping herself up in a rich Kashmere, 'that there is some way of knowing a thing that cost fifty guineas from an article that is sold for five; but I venture to say there are not one out of ten thousand that would understand the difference.'

Few of the so-called 'Thibet shawls' were really woven in goat-fleece, although to reach the true facts in this connection is made difficult by the secrecy with which the search for substitutes was conducted by individual firms concerned. One of the leading Paisley manufacturers of the day, Messrs Millar & Sons, went to the extreme of building a special factory outside the town where they could experiment without fear of spying.[1]

The 'Thibet shawl' was a square shawl with plain centre, surrounded by applied borders in four or five colours. From an examination of those which survive, it is possible to conclude that there were two main kinds. One of these combined silk warps with wefts spun from a mixture of fine wool and silk waste; the other had a field of fine Australian wool which was known as 'Botany worsted', apparently woven in Yorkshire.[2] The decorative borders of both kinds were woven at Paisley with silk warps and woollen wefts and subsequently applied to the fields. Of the two kinds, the latter was perhaps the more common; and it is significant that at least one Paisley authority was in the habit of using 'Thibet wool' and 'Botany worsted' as synonymous terms.[3]

The years 1825–40 marked the period when Paisley challenged and finally outstripped Norwich in the British shawl trade. This success was achieved not merely as the result of deliberate pirating and underselling, but more particularly because of Paisley's more advanced methods of manufacture. Division of labour, for instance, was more advanced at Paisley. The production of a shawl no longer depended upon simple negotiation between manufacturer and weaver: instead, independent specialists were involved at every stage.

---

[1] *Paisley Herald*, 12th November, 1859.

[2] *New Statistical Account of Scotland*, vol. VII, 1845.

[3] Matthew Blair, p. 83.

First, a Paisley design was sketched on plain white paper by the pattern-drawer and then transferred to squared or 'point' paper, with lines representing individual warps and wefts. This was then handed to the 'fluer-lasher' who, with the help of a frame designed for the purpose, made up the 'bridle' which was required to manipulate the warps. Next, there was the 'harness-tier' whose job was to set up the harness; then the 'enterer', who passed the threads through the heddles; the 'warp-stainer', who stained the warps according to pattern; and the 'beamer', who fixed the warps in the loom. After weaving, the shawl passed through the hands of a clipper, who cut off the floating wefts on the reverse side,[1] and other specialists responsible for fringing, finishing and pressing.[2]

It must be admitted that increased technical efficiency in some respects was off-set by a falling off of standards in others. For instance, in the early Paisley shawls there is a unity of texture between figure-work and ground, which is rarely found in the shawls of the 1830s and later. Decline was due to the employment of coarser yarns for the figure-work: whereas formerly coloured weft yarns had been from 36 to 50 hanks to the pound, they were now only from 14 to 24 hanks. This use of coarser yarn was encouraged by manufacturers, because weavers were paid according to the number of wefts in a fabric, and fewer wefts meant cheaper costs.

A contemporary writer mentions a further technical improvement which had an important influence on Paisley shawls of the period. It was called the 'double ground or two backs', which enabled 'more colouring to be thrown into the pattern, as well as a saving to be effected in the cost of production.'[3] Although the writer does not elaborate further, Mr J. F. Flanagan, a distinguished authority on weaving history, to whom I have shown this passage, suggests the following explanation, communicated to me in a letter: ' "Two backs" must mean that there were two ground warps which were mainly at the back of the cloth and brought to the surface as required. Only one of the warps would be on the surface at any part of the surface, unless a mixed warp effect was required at a particular part of the ground. I think it certain that the ground warps would be of two colours. Therefore there would be the advantage of two ground colours instead of the normal one. The saving in production would be that two ground

---

[1] In 1834, a machine, invented in France, was introduced for clipping. *New Statistical Account of Scotland*, 1845, p. 266.

[2] *Report from Assistant Handloom Weavers' Commissioners*, pt. 1, p. 33.

[3] Anonymous, *Paisley—the Shawl Trade*, p. 215. The same writer mentions another technical improvement as 'the tweeling of the spotting or colours which form the pattern'; but I am uncertain of the precise meaning here.

colours could be brought to the surface, each as required, for a single weft pick.'

At this period there were three main types or sizes of shawl. First, the *plaid*, which measured about twelve feet by five feet; secondly, the *three-quarter plaid*, about eight feet by five feet; and thirdly, the shawl proper, about six feet square. The *plaid* owed its size to the fact that it was intended to be folded double and worn as a square. A *shawl*, on the other hand, was folded diagonally and worn with the downward apex at the back. In order to show off all four borders, two of them were usually reversed, the reason for which is only apparent when the shawl is folded (*see* Plates 42 and 43).

About 1840 Paisley introduced the so-called 'patent double-shawl' or 'back-to-back' style (not to be confused with the Jacquard-woven reversible shawl of the 1860s which will be discussed later). The 'patent double-shawl' consisted of two shawls woven simultaneously back-to-back, the redundant wefts being concealed between the two surfaces.[1] The patterns on the two sides were complementary, the ground on one side corresponding to the figure-work on the other, and vice-versa. Although considerable skill must have gone into the making of the double-shawls on an ordinary draw-loom, they could never have been very popular on account of their weight. An example at Paisley Museum weighs 9½ lbs and is perhaps typical.

The most important of all technical advances in shawl-weaving, of which Paisley was the quickest to take advantage, was the introduction from France of the Jacquard machine. Operations which had previously depended upon one or more drawboys working with the weaver were now automatically directed by perforated cards, on the same principle as the barrel-organ or pianola. The actual harness of the loom worked as before, but the weaver's task was greatly simplified, particularly in the weaving of elaborate patterns. Instead of the 'fluer-lasher', a new class of specialists known as 'card-cutters', came into being, their job being to punch holes in the cards required for the Jacquard machine.

The Jacquard machine (*see* Illus. No. 7, facing p. 27) first reached Paisley in 1833 or 1834.[2] Even there, however, its adoption was slow, partly due to technical imperfections, only slowly overcome; and partly because few weavers could afford the capital outlay required for installation of the new loom and equipment. Although manufacturers were often willing to advance money for purchase, the weaver still had to face a loss in time required for its setting up, and

---

[1] Anonymous, *Paisley—the Shawl Trade*, p. 217; and W. Cross, p. 18. The latter attributes the introduction of the double-shawl to the 1820s but is probably wrong. A. M. Stewart (p. 21) confuses the early double-shawl with the later reversible, the latter being woven on a different principle.

[2] *Report from Assistant Handloom Weavers' Commissioners*, pt. 1, 1839, p. 309.

in mastery of its technique. At first Jacquard looms were probably used only for the borders of plain shawls, and not until about 1845 was it described as being in *general* use for shawl weaving.[1]

The introduction of the Jacquard was of more than technical significance: it marked the beginning of French domination in British shawl design. It is impossible to discuss the later history of Paisley shawls apart from shawl history in France.

THE SHAWL IN FRANCE

Little mention has so far been made of the French industry because the shawl came into vogue later in France than in England. As late as 1788, genuine *kashmirs* sent from India as presents to French women were cut up for petticoats instead of being used as intended.[2] The earliest illustration of a woollen shawl being worn in France appears in a fashion magazine dated June, 1790, whence it was described as an *English* fashion (*toilette à l'anglaise*).[3] French writers usually attribute its general adoption in France to Napoleon's Egyptian campaign (1798–1801), when officers serving with the forces are said to have sent home shawls to their womenfolk. However, it is more likely that demand preceded supply, and this would certainly have been consistent with the needs of contemporary fashion. French women, in order to show their figures to better advantage, had discarded the cloak, and a substitute warmer than silk was needed to replace it. For this purpose the *kashmir* was admirably suited. Henchforth a lady was described not as 'well dressed' but as 'well draped', and the draping of a shawl became an art to be learnt from professional instructresses, a number of whom advertised in Parish fashion journals of the period. A leader of the new fashion was the Empress Josephine. Contemporary records tell us that she possessed between three and four hundred shawls, some of which she had made into gowns, bed-quilts, and even cushions for her dog.[4] From the same source one learns that Napoleon, preferring to see her shoulders uncovered, sometimes pulled off the shawl she was wearing and flung it into the fire, whereupon the Empress would calmly send to her wardrobe for another.

The first French imitations were made in 1804. These were woven in a harness-loom similar to that in use at Norwich. They had silk warps and woollen wefts,

---

[1] *Paisley Herald*, 12th November, 1859.

[2] Legoux de Flaix, p. 294; J. Rey, p. 146, and Racinet, vi, p. 36.

[3] *Journal de la Mode et du Goût*, Paris, June, 1790. Reproduced by J. Grand-Carteret, pl. 26.

[4] *Memoirs of Madame de Rémusat*, 1802–8, vol. 2, pp. 108–9.

and sometimes as many as six colours.[1] A public exhibition held at the Palais-Bourbon in 1806 included two types of shawl, described by a witness as follows: '. . . un châle de cinq quarts carré, à bordures de dix-huit lignes, orné d'une petite rosace au milieu, brochée à peu de couleurs; et un châle long, fond blanc, dessin imité du cachemire sur une chaîne de soie, tramé et broché en laine. La bordure avait environ neuf lignes, et était sans guirlande. Elle n'était point accompagnée de ces palmettes de coins, qui aujourd'hui (1823) paraissent l'ornement indispensable des bordures en ruban, nommées *talon*. Les grandes palmes des extrémités étaient hautes de neuf pouces seulement, parce que les palmes des cachemires de cette époque n'avaient aussi que cette élévation.[2] Cette exposition donna un grand essor a la fabrique de châles.'[3] Examples of both types of shawl described here appear frequently in contemporary French fashion plates and are easily identifiable.[4]

The prices of *kashmirs* in France at this period varied from 1,700 to 3,000 francs each; but no lady of fashion was content with merely one or two, which meant that there was no limit to what some were ready to spend. When Napoleon married Marie Louise he made her an allowance of 80,000 francs solely for the purchase of 'les châles et dentelles'.[5] But whereas the supremacy of the real *kashmir* has always been admitted in England, there was less willingness to admit this in France. Admiring the true *kashmir* primarily for its warmth and softness of texture, French manufacturers always thought that in the field of design there was scope for improvement. With this end in view, two of the leading manufacturers petitioned Napoleon's Minister of the Interior. Announcing their intention of producing shawl designs 'more in conformity with French taste', they asked for official encouragement. 'We wish that His Majesty would acquire twelve only to give as presents to ladies of the Court. We do not doubt that by this means they would be keenly sought after, that the mode would take hold of Paris all the more easily, and from there the whole of Europe, that taste frequently changes where this type of article is concerned, and that people are beginning to get tired of the Indian *palmes* [i.e. cones] without tiring of the article itself . . . Your Excellency will make even more certain the success of our plans if he approaches one of His Majesty's painters, Isabey, whose style is well known,

[1] J. Rey, p. 195.
[2] This statement is apparently not accurate, for it is contradicted by the evidence of the portrait of Mme Rivière at Plate 6.
[3] J. Rey, pp. 196–7.
[4] J. Grand-Carteret, especially plates 99, 100, 103, 108 and 111. For the manner of wearing shawls at this period, see also Racinet, vi, p. 33.
[5] A. Maze-Sencier, p. 313.

asking him to negotiate with us over the choice of designs.'[1] These proposals met with prompt response. Isabey and several other distinguished artists of the day consented to produce designs, and on 31st December, 1812, twelve shawls of 'improved design' were accepted by the Empress Marie Louise, who kept some for herself and gave the remainder to her ladies-in-waiting. The latter are said to have obliged by carrying them about ostentaciously, with the result that at first their entourage, and then all Paris society, began to follow. A few weeks later the press announced a triumph of the new style. 'The shawls of MM. Ternaux are a perfect product. The designs are the work of our best artists and they are different from the bizarre and confused designs that one finds on the foreign [i.e. Kashmir] shawls. The *palmes* [i.e. cones] are replaced by bouquets and garlands imitating the most beautiful European flowers whose clear colours and fine nuances have something of the appearance of painting . . .'[2]

Unfortunately, none of these particular shawls is known to have survived; but the story is none the less significant as an illustration of the importance attached by the French, even at this early period, to design. In 1835 it was said that French shawl manufacturers were spending as much as 10 per cent of their gross capital on the preparation of new designs.[3] Their lead in this respect was acknowledged by British manufacturers, and from 1840 onwards the French *kashmir*, rather than the true *kashmir*, was taken as the model in Britain.[4]

Besides the superiority of designs, two other factors contributed to the domination of French influence. First, they had had longer experience with the Jacquard machine and were therefore ahead in developing the elaborate types of pattern appropriate to it. Secondly, a lifting of import restrictions on silks in 1829 resulted in a flood of 'rich figured French shawls' into Britain, and their adoption in fashionable circles.[5]

PAISLEY: THE FINAL PHASE, 1840–70

By 1840, Paisley had begun to copy French designs in earnest, and more and more Jacquard looms were installed for the purpose. Designs characteristic of the

[1] Letter from the brothers Ternaux to Montalivet, Minister of the Interior, dated 28.5.1811, quoted L. Lomuller, *Existe-t-il des châles Ternaux dessinés par Isabey?*, Beaux Arts, Paris, 15th April, 1949, No. 120.
[2] *Moniteur Universel*, Paris, 1st February, 1813, quoted by L. Lomuller, *Ibid.*
[3] *Report from House of Commons Select Committee on Handloom Weavers*, 1835, para. 177.
[4] 'Lyons beats us, and indeed the rest of the world, chiefly by the superiority of her patterns, and the excellence of taste displayed in designs.' *Report from Assistant Handloom Weavers' Commissioners*, pt. II, 1839, p. 123. 'Since beginning the use of the Jacquard loom, our countrymen have scarcely done more than copy the French.' Anonymous, *Paisley—the Shawl Trade*, p. 216.
[5] *Report from the H. of C. Select Committee on Handloom Weavers*, 1834, paras. 1160 and 6976.

1840s were distinguished by elongated, multiple cones running from edge to centre and leaving only about half the centre-field plain. This style was derived almost entirely from pattern-books printed and published in Paris, many of which found their way to Paisley—some being yet preserved at Paisley Museum.

The trend towards greater elaboration culminated in the 1850s with the introduction from France of the all-over patterned shawl. In this, the whole ground is figured with the exception of a small area in the centre. These shawls were usually of the *plaid* shape, sometimes exceeding twelve feet in length. Individual repeat units of the design sometimes covered as much as a quarter of the whole ground, and their intricacy of detail marked the final triumph of the Jacquard machine.

At this stage, French manufacturers were becoming sensitive to the pirating of their designs by Paisley, and it is interesting to find that one French firm went to the trouble of having its designs registered at the British Patent Office.[1]

To some extent individuality had been expressed in Paisley designs by the introduction of naturalistic floral motives, and Paisley shawls with designs of this kind were shown at the Great Exhibition of 1851.[2] It can hardly be argued, however, that this treatment represented an advance on French design: more often than not the naturalism was vulgar and sentimental, reminiscent of the worst features of early Victorian decorative art.

In the 1850s and 1860s an extremely complex situation was reached in the international shawl trade. On the one hand, the Kashmir industry was largely under the domination of French merchants who had settled there, bringing with them their own pattern-books for the native designers to copy. At the same time, France was producing imitation *kashmirs* which were often a decade ahead of the Indian-made designs they were supposed to be imitating, and these in turn were being copied or adapted by Paisley weavers. In spite of all this, the idea of a genuine *kashmir* as opposed to a European imitation still retained its associations of superiority, and this explains why some Jacquard weavers in the West went as far as to simulate Persian lettering on their shawls, to give them an added note of authenticity. An example of a Paisley shawl with a fake Persian inscription is shown at Plate 46.

The last innovation introduced at Paisley was the *reversible* shawl (Plate 33), which probably came as an answer to the reversible shawls of Kashmir, first made about 1865 (Plate 33). Paisley reversibles were made on the Jacquard loom with a double set of warps, the repeat sections of the pattern being ingeniously

---

[1] The firm was Steinbach Koechlin & Co., of Mulhouse. Patent Office, Class VII, Book X, *passim.*

[2] *Illustrated Catalogue of the Great Exhibition*, 1851, pp. 55, 157 and 254.

composed so that opposite sides of the cloth were complementary to one another. The redundant wefts threads, when not engaged in the pattern on either face of the cloth, were left floating between the two surfaces. Unlike the 'patent double-shawls' of the 1840s, which were described earlier, the pattern was so designed that there were extremely few floating wefts, the majority being taken up on one surface or the other. A reversible shawl was intended to be worn unfolded, with the same effect as a folded *plaid*, and for this reason it did not require to be more than half the length.

As explained in the first chapter, the Franco-Prussian War (1870–1) marked the eclipse of the shawl as an article of fashion in the West. More accurately, it should be said that it marked its eclipse as a *luxury* fashion only, for one of the factors which contributed to its abandonment in upper-class circles was undoubtedly its increasing popularity among the lower classes. By 1870, a Jacquard-woven Paisley shawl could be bought for as little as £1,[1] and the identical pattern printed on cotton cost only a very few shillings. Thus, the Kashmir style, originally a mark of exclusiveness and exotic rarity, had now become vulgar and mundane as a result of its popularity. The surprising thing is that this process took as long as a hundred years.

---

[1] In 1860, the *average* price of a large Paisley harness shawl was 27s, and the cheapest were 17s 6d. Paisley Museum and Art Gallery, *Letters and other papers relating to the evidence given to the Conseil Supérieur* . . . (*see* Bibliography under MSS.).

APPENDIX I

*An account of Shawl-Goods produced in Kashmir in 1823
Compiled from Moorcroft MSS. E.113 and D.264[1]*

TRADE NAME	REMARKS	MANUFAC-TURER'S PRICE	MARKETS
Do-Shāla (or shawls in pairs)			
Pattū pashmīna	Sometimes made of *asli tūs*, but more often of the coarser kinds of shawl wool. Length 4 *gaz*, breadth 1½ *gaz*.[2] This is thick and is used as a blanket or for outer clothing	From 5 to 6 rupees per *gaz*	Kashmir, Afghanistan
Shāla phīri	As its name denotes, it is made of *phīri* or seconds wool. Length from 3½ to 4 *gaz*, breadth 1½ *gaz*	From 20 to 30 rupees per piece	Kashmir
Hulwān	Plain white cloth of fine shawl-wool without flower border or other ornament, differs in length but is 12 *girahs* in[3] breadth and is used for turbans and for dyeing	From 3 to 6 rupees per *gaz*	Kashmir, Hindustan, Persia, Afghanistan, etc.
Jauhar shāla sada	A shawl with a narrow edging of coloured yarn. From 3½ to 3¾ *gaz* in length, and 1½ in breadth	From 50 to 60 rupees per piece[4]	Kashmir, Hindustan, etc.
Shāla hāshiyadār	Edged by a single border. 3½ *gaz* in length, and 1½ *gaz* in breadth	From 60 to 70 rupees per piece	Kashmir, Hindustan, etc.
Shāla do-hāshiyadār	With a double border. Same measurements	From 40 or 60 to 70 rupees per piece	Kashmir, Hindustan, etc.

---

[1] I am indebted to Mr R. W. Skelton, Assistant at the Indian Section, Victoria and Albert Museum, for help in the revision of transliterations.

[2] The standard, or *ilāhi*, *gaz* was 33 inches.

[3] A *girah* was one-sixteenth of a yard.

[4] MSS. Eur. D. 264 reads 'per pair'.

TRADE NAME	REMARKS	MANUFAC-TURER'S PRICE	MARKETS
Shāla chahār hāshiyadār	With four borders. Same measurements	From 60 to 70 rupees per piece	Kashmir, Hindustan, etc.
Hāshiyadār khosar or *Khalīl khānī*	With two borders and two tunga, sometimes with, at others without, a flower in the corners. Same measurements	From 40 to 50 rupees per piece	Afghanistan
Hāshiyadār kunguradār	This has a border of unusual form with another within side, or nearer to the middle, resembling the crest of the Wall of Asiatic forts furnished with narrow niches or embrasures for Wall pieces, or Matchlocks, whence its name. Same measurements	From 100 to 150 rupees a pair	Hindustan, etc.
Daurdār	With an ornament running all round the shawl between the border and the field. Same measurements	From 100 to 2,300 rupees a pair	Hindustan, Russia
Matandār	With flowers or decorations in the middle of the field. Same measurements	From 300 to 1,800 rupees a pair	Hindustan, Turkey
Chand-dār	With a circular ornament or moon in the centre of the field. Same measurements	From 500 to 2,500 rupees a pair	Hindustan, Turkey, etc.
Chauthidār	With four half-moons. Same measurements	From 300 to 1,500 rupees a pair	Hindustan
Kunjbūṭedār	With a group of flowers at each corner. Same measurements	From 200 to 900 rupees a pair	Hindustan, Afghanistan, Persia
Alifdār	With green sprigs without any other colour on a white ground. Same measurements	From 120 to 150 rupees a pair	Hindustan, but more especially Peerzadas [*sic*]
Kuddhar	With large groups of flowers somewhat in the form of the cone of a pine with the ends or points straight or curved downwards. Same measurements	—	—

TRADE NAME	REMARKS	MANUFAC-TURER'S PRICE	MARKETS
Do-kuddhar	With two rows of such groups. Same measurements	From 100 to 800 ruppees a pair	Hindustan
Se-kuddhar	With three rows of the same	From 100 to 800 rupees a pair	Hindustan
Chahar-kuddhar	With four rows of the same[1]	From 200 to 600 rupees a pair	Hindustan
Jāmawārs (or gown-pieces)	Sold in lengths of $3\frac{3}{4}$ *gaz* by $1\frac{1}{2}$ *gaz*		
Khukhabutha (*Kokā-būṭā* ?)	Large compound flowers, consisting of groups of smaller ones	From 300 to 1,500 rupees per piece	Used by the Persians and Afghans
Rezabūṭā	Small flowers thickly set	From 200 to 700 rupees per piece	Kashmir, Hindustan, Afghanistan
Jāl-dār	Net-work	From 500 to 1,700 rupees per piece	Persia, Turkey, Turkistan, Afghanistan
Islimi	——	From 250 to 400 rupees per per piece	Kashmir, Turkistan. To Persia for saddlecloths, curtains, and women's use
Maramat	——	From 150 to 300 rupees per piece	Kashmir, Afghanistan, Persia
Khutherast (*Khatārāst* ?)	——	From 150 to 750 rupees a piece	Kashmir, Persia, Afghanistan, Turkistan
Marpih	——	From 200 to 350 rupees a piece	Kashmir, Persia, Afghanistan, Turkistan

[1] Here Moorcroft adds: ' . . . and so on to five and upwards. In the latter case, however, the cones are somewhat small.'

TRADE NAME	REMARKS	MANUFAC-TURER'S PRICE	MARKETS
Qalam-kār	——	From 300 to 1,000 rupees a piece	Bokhara, Russia, Con-stantinople (but not large)
Tāk-i-angūr	——	From 300 to 500 rupees a piece	Deccan, few to Turkistan
Chap-o-rast	——	From 300 to 700 rupees a piece	Afghanistan, Persia, Baghdad
Do-gul	——	From 500 to 1,000 rupees a piece	Persia, Con-stantinople, Baghdad
Burghabad	——	From 250 to 400 rupees a piece	Kashmir, a little in Hindustan, much in Persia and Afghanistan
Gulasaut	——	From 200 to 900 rupees a piece	Afghanistan, Persia
Dawāzda-khat	——	From 200 to 900 rupees a piece	Turkistan, Turkey, Persia
Dawāzda-rang	——	From 800 to 1,400 rupees a piece	Turkey
Goole parwane (Gul-o-parvāna ?)	——	From 300 to 450 rupees a piece	Yarkand

TRADE NAME	REMARKS	MANUFAC-TURER'S PRICE	MARKETS
Kayehamoo (*Ka'i-amau'a* ?) *sabz-kār safīd*	These are made by the shawl-weaver alone and go largely into Hindustan where they are dyed, the small green flowers being previously tied up in hard small knots so as to be protected from the action of the dye, and are of course when untied each surrounded by a small white field. Small eyes of spots of yellow, red and of other colours are supposed to harmonize with the green flowers and the new ground, and these are added by embroiderers or *chikān-doz*	From 120 to 130 rupees a piece	—
Qasaba or Rūmāl (woman's veil or square shawl)	1½ to 2½ *gaz* square	—	—
Khat-dār	——	From 300 to 500 rupees a piece	Hindustan
Māramat	——	From 150 to 300 rupees a piece	Afghanistan, Persia, Turkey
Islimi (with 13 other *Jāmawār* patterns)	——	From 150 to 300 rupees a piece	Afghanistan, Turkey, Persia, Turkistan
Chahār-bāgh	——	From 300 to 350 rupees a piece	Turkey, Russia, a few to Hindustan
Do-hāshiya	——	From 100 to 175 rupees a piece	Hindustan, a few to Persia
Chand-dār	——	From 50 to 200 rupees a piece	Kashmir, Afghanistan, Turkistan, few to Persia
Chouthidār	——	From 150 to 400 rupees	Persia, Hindustan, Turkey, Baghdad, Turkistan

TRADE NAME	REMARKS	MANUFAC-TURER'S PRICE	MARKETS
Shash chouthidār	——	From 250 to 500 rupees	Persia, Hindustan, few to Turkey
Farangi	——	From 100 to 500 rupees	Exported chiefly to Russia
Tarah–armani	——·	From 100 to 250 rupees a piece	Exported chiefly to Armenia, also Turkey
Tarah–rūmāl	——	From 120 to 200 rupees	Exported chiefly to Turkey, a few to Turkistan
Sāda (plain)	——	From 12 to 15 rupees	Kashmir (for domestic use)
Shamlas (Girdles for the waist, worn by Asiatics)	These are 8 *gaz* in length and 1½ *gaz* broad, and of various colours and patterns. They vary from 50 to 2,000 rupees in price according to the richness of their work	—	—
Sāda (plain)	——	From 50 to 70 rupees a piece	Kashmir, Kabul, Afghanistan, a few to Turkistan
Hāshiya-dār	——	From 70 to 200 rupees a piece	Kashmir, Kabul, Afghanistan, a few to Turkistan
Phalā-dār	With two *phalās* and two *hāshiyas* (see Glossary). Grounds of different kinds, as with flowers, lines, sprigs, etc.—viz.:	—	—
Matanbāgh	All flowers	From 500 to 2,000 rupees a piece	Persia
Lahri-dār	Waved like water	From 300 to 1,000 rupees a piece	Persia, Turkey, Baghdad

TRADE NAME	REMARKS	MANUFAC-TURER'S PRICE	MARKETS
Khānchā-dār	In trays or plates	From 1,000 to 1,700 rupees a piece	Persia, Turkistan, Turkey, a few to Afghanistan
Māramat	Snaky	From 200 to 1,300 rupees a piece	Persia, a few to Turkey
Rāh-dār	Running between parallel lines	From 300 to 800 rupees a piece	Afghanistan, a few to Turkistan and India
Do-shāla se phalā-dār (shawls with three heads)	This variety contains three *phalās* (see Glossary) instead of two and goes only to Tibet	From 100 to 150 rupees a piece	—
Gospech or Patkā, or Turbans	Length from 8 to 10 *gaz*, breadth 1 *gaz*, and of all colours. One variety has two *phalās*, two *tanjirs*, and two *hāshiyas* (see Glossary). Another variety, *Mandila*, sometimes has a *tanjir* and sometimes not. This is from 8 to 10 *gaz* in length and about 12 *girahs* in breadth	From 150 to 800 rupees From 45 to 70 rupees	— —
Khalin pashmīna (shawl carpets)	These are sold per square *gaz* and are made of any size in a single piece	From 20 to 40 rupees per square *gaz*	—
Naqsh or Trousers	Some are with, others without seams. The former are made of two pieces which are sewn together by the *rafūgar*, the latter by the *jarrāb-doz* or stocking-maker	From 200 to 500 rupees a pair	—
Chahārkhāna or Netted Cloth	Used by women. Length indefinite, breadth from 14 *girahs*	From 5 to 10 rupees a piece	Persia, Hindustan, a few to Afghanistan, and a few in Kashmir
Gul-badan	Length indefinite, breadth from 14 *girahs* to 1 *gaz*	From 5 to 6 rupees a *gaz*	Persia, Afghanistan, New Shah Jahan
Lungi or Girdles	These differ from *shamlas* by being in narrow check and bordered by lines of different colours. L. 3½ *gaz*, W. 1½ *gaz*	From 50 to 75 rupees a piece	Kashmir, Persia

TRADE NAME	REMARKS	MANUFAC-TURER'S PRICE	MARKETS
Takhin or Caps	——	From 8 annas to 4 rupees	Kashmir, few to Kabul and Hindustan
Jarrāb or Short Stockings	Flowered and striped in the *guldār* and *māramat* styles	From 1 to 5 rupees	Kashmir, Hindustan, Kabul, Persia, few to Turkey
Moza Pashmīna or Long Stockings	——	From 5 to 25 rupees a piece	Hindustan, Persia, Turkey, Turkistan, Russia
Sakkabposh (Sāqibposh ?)	——	From 300 to 1,500 rupees	Persia, Turkey, Arabia
Darparda or Curtains (for doors or windows)	——	The price the same as Jamawar, sold according to measure	Persia, Turkey, Arabia, Russia
Kajjari asp or Saddle-cloth	——	The price the same as Jamawar, sold according to measure	Persia
Kajjari fil or Elephant's housing	——	The price the the same as Jamawar, sold according to measure	Hindustan
Bālāposh or Palangposh (quilts or coverlets)	——	From 300 to 1,000 rupees	Turkistan, Persia, Turkey, Russia, a few to Afghanistan
Galāband or Cravat	——	From 12 to 300 rupees	Hindustan
Pistānband or Neckerchief	——	From 5 to 15 rupees	Kashmir, Afghanistan, Persia, Hindustan

TRADE NAME	REMARKS	MANUFAC-TURER'S PRICE	MARKETS
Langota or Waist Belts	——	From 15 to 30 rupees	Persia, Afghanistan, a few to Turkistan
Postīn (cloths left long in the Nap to line pelisses)	——	From 500 to 1,000 rupees	Persia
Pāipech or Leggings	Length 2 *gaz*, breadth 1 *girah*. Of all colours	From 2 to 10 rupees	Kabul, Kandahar, Turkistan, Turkey, Persia
Izārband or Waist Strings	——	From 1 to 15 rupees each	Persia, Afghanistan
Takīn or Pillow-bier	——	The price the same as Jamawar	Persia, Russia, Turkey, Arabia, Hindustan
Khalīta (bags or purses)	——	From 8 annas to 2 rupees	Kashmir, Kabul
Qabr-posh or Shrouds (for tombs)	——	The price the same as Jamawar	Persia, Arabia, Turkistan
Tāqposh (covers or hangings for recesses, cupboards, etc.)	——	The price the same as Jamawar	Persia

APPENDIX II

Moorcroft's proposals for the emigration of Kashmiri weavers, spinners and pattern-drawers and their settlement in Britain[1]

1. Excerpt from a letter from Moorcroft to Mr C. T. Metcalfe, the East India Company's Resident at Delhi, written at Amritsar, 21st May, 1820 (MSS. Eur.F.38).

'. . . I beg to submit to you in relation to the growing importance of the Shawl Trade in Britain and the obvious advantage of obtaining an early superiority in the manufacture of the article, from the process of picking and cleaning the raw material to that of packing shawls in Bales, which in Britain is ill-conducted, it would not be prudent to invite as many Kashmeerees to proceed to Britain as would be able to go through all the processes employed in this manufacture. The argument of the expense of this measure can only be estimated by a comparison of the merits of Kashmeeree and of English artists, a point not yet wholly adjusted, but the absolute expense will not be great considering the present low wages of the spinners and weavers.

The English borrowed the art of printing Chintz from the artists of this country and now surpass their teachers, and a similar event may reasonably be expected in regard to shawls, if the British manufacturers be sufficiently attentive to their real interests, and not suffer immediate profits by cheapness, to delude them from possessing a paramount and permanent command of the market by superiority of manufacture.

Through a complete set of Kashmeeree Shawl Artists the English manufacturers will *per saltum* seize the advantages of the science and manipulation the experience of centuries has supplied to that branch of manufacture, which, through local circumstances, has been favoured and fostered into a most profitable and most extensive trade, supporting many thousands of individuals, and for rivalry in which several European Nations are now contending. When the English Manufacturers shall have gained the whole Mystery of those Artists who are now confessedly the best performers, let them engraft their own improvements, but let them now start with all 'appliances and means to boot'.

---

[1] Proposals for the emigration of Kashmiri weavers and their settlement under French patronage on the island of Madagascar had been published in 1792 by the Abbé Rochon (*Voyage to Madagascar*), but Moorcroft was apparently unaware of this.

English pride of science may be startled at the supposition that any Oriental Workman can excel English Artisans in manufacturing articles on which English industry has long employed its powers, but such presumption arrests the progress of art, and candour must acknowledge superiority in the material, fabric and temper of some of the Sword blades and Gun barrels of the East: I propose to bring on my return some Gun barrels from Lahor for inspection by British Gunsmiths and which cannot fail to astonish them by their beauty.

Luminously satisfactory and abundant as in latter years have been the reasonings and deductions on colours and on mordants and expeditious and cheap, the modes of extracting and applying colouring matters, it will perhaps be found that industry and long practice, stimulated by the desire of gain, have attained a progress in the art of dyeing woollens *permanently* in Kashmeer, that may not yield in general result, to the lucubrations and discoveries affected by experimental philosophy applied to the same object in Europe.

I must request the favour of your obtaining the sentiments of Mr Reding on the matter of inviting some Kashmeerees to emigrate, and if they be favourable, that you will bring it under the notice of the Government, as expeditiously as possible, in any shape you may think fit.

Amongst the many thousands of individuals employed in the Shawl trade in Kashmeer, it would probably be no difficult task to induce two or three families in a noiseless way to leave that country, but I submit to you that it would be more proper, as an affair in which the Government take an interest, to ask Runjeet Singh to allow me to do this publicly, in passing through Kashmeer.

A belief that the water of Kashmeer is essential to produce good shawls, and that such is not to be met with elsewhere, will prevent apprehensions of rivalry. If this measure be determined upon a letter under cover to Khooshwant Rau, the newswriter, directing him to forward it to me by Qasid, will reach me. And in such event I must further beg that you will cause it to be accompanied by a letter of Credit or Bill for two thousand rupees to be employed by me in relieving the pecuniary embarrassments of some families in distress, for such will be the fittest subjects for experiment, and for furnishing way expenses.

Pattern drawers will of course be included in the detail of Artists from possessing the peculiar patterns of Kashmeer, which for a time may be preferred in Europe to those of that country.

There is nothing novel in such transplantation of artists. Louis XV procured Workmen in Muslins from India, but through the negligence of his Ministers many of them perished through want. And Catherine II invited great numbers of Artists in the Silk Trade, from Lyons, who had formed a Manufactory of

Brocades, that now supplies most of the north-western parts of Asia with this 'Article'.

2. Excerpt from Moorcroft's notes written in Kashmir, 4th February, 1823 (MSS. Eur.D.264, pp. 43–4):

'It might border on extravagance to advocate the employment of the labour of the hand on an occupation advantageously superseded by machinery of the most efficient description for preparing thread suited for most fabrics of cloth. But if it be a fact as reported that machinery cannot furnish your yarn as well adapted for the manufacture of Shawls as that spun by hand in Kashmeer nothing would be more easy than to induce a few Kashmeeree families to proceed to Britain on very light terms of remuneration. Whether the introduction of the mode of spinning yarn for shawl-cloth would afford much occupation to weakly and indigent females in Britain is competently to be appreciated by individuals now in that country, but on such a presumption the art might be readily diffused. An unsuccessful experiment was made many years ago at the suggestion, it is believed, of Dupleix or of Le Comte de Lally to import fabrics of India, for the purpose of establishing a manufacture of Muslins in France. Emigrants suffered much from the climate, and after having experienced in Paris a reception and treatment not exactly corresponding to that they were thought to expect they were furnished with an Asylum in one of the Grecian islands where drawings of the occupations were taken by the late Mr Tresham and are presumed to be in the possession of the Right Hon. Lord Cawdor. Nothing in the climate of Britain is likely to prove unfriendly to the constitution of Kashmeerees, for at this moment in Kashmeer (Feb. 4th) the thermometer out of doors stands at twenty-four degrees.'

GLOSSARY OF TERMS USED IN KASHMIR
SHAWL-WEAVING

'Amli, 'amlikar. Needlework shawl. From Persian *'amli,* 'worked'.

'Asli tūs. The true Kashmiri name of the best shawl-wool, derived from a Central Asian species of the wild mountain goat, *Capra hircus.*

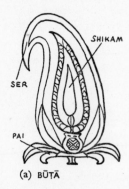

(a) BŪTĀ

Būṭā. Generic term for the cone, meaning literally 'flower' (see fig. a).

Daur. The running ornament sometimes enveloping the field of a shawl on the inside of the *hāshiya and tanjir.*

Do-shāla. A pair of shawls.

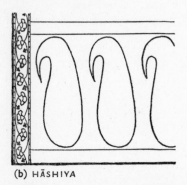

(b) HĀSHIYA

Hāshiya. The narrow-patterned border running down the sides of a shawl (see fig. b).

(c) JHĀL

Jhāl. The decoration which sometimes fills the ground between the cones in the heads of a shawl (see fig. c). It means literally 'net'.

Kanikar. Loom-woven shawl. See also *Tilikar.*

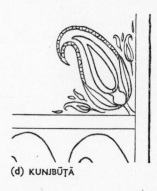

(d) KUNJBŪṬĀ

Kunjbūṭā. Corner ornament (usually a cone) sometimes found in each corner of the field (see fig. d).

Kārkhānadār. The owner of a shawl manufactory.

Kasawa, or Kasaba. A square shawl. See also *Rūmāl.*

Lungi. A girdle. See also *Shamla.*

(e) MATAN

Matan. The main field of a shawl (see fig. e).
Mohkun. Shawl-broker.
Naqqāsh. Pattern-drawer.
Pāi. The foot or pediment of a cone (see fig. a).
Pashmīna. The name applied in the West to true Kashmiri shawl-cloth. From Persian *pashm*, 'wool'.

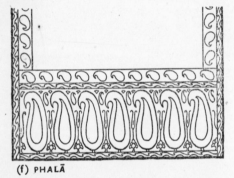

(f) PHALĀ

Phalā. The large-patterned border at each end, or head, of a shawl (see fig. f).

Phīri. Seconds yarn.
Rafūgar. Embroiderer and darner.
Rūmāl. Square shawl.
Ser. The head of tip of a cone (see fig. a).
Shamla. A girdle. See also *Lungi.*
Shikam. The belly of a cone (see fig. a).
Ta'līm-gurū. Pattern-master, responsible for transcribing the colour-pattern into short-hand.

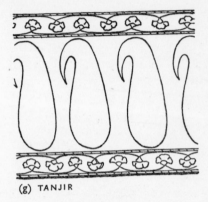

(g) TANJIR

Tanjir. The narrow-patterned border which runs above and below the *phalā*, confining it (see fig. g).
Tarah-gurū. Colour-caller.
Tilikar. Loom-woven shawl. See also *kanikar.*
Tojli. The spool used for threading the coloured weft threads of loom-woven shawls.
Ustād. Master-weaver, applied loosely to all loom-owners, and in the late nineteenth century to overseers at the manufactories.

BIBLIOGRAPHY

THE following list of works quoted in the text is not intended as a guide to further reading. For students seeking the latter, a few general comments may be helpful.

For Kashmir shawl history, the most important source is the Moorcroft MSS. written between 1820 and 1823, now preserved at the India Office Library (see under *Manuscripts*). A précis of these manuscripts is included in H. H. Wilson's posthumous compilation, *Travels in the Himalayan Provinces of Hindustan and the Punjab . . . by W. Moorcroft and G. Trebeck* (two vols, London, 1841). Wilson's précis, however, which has hitherto been the only source used in quoting Moorcroft on shawl history, is arbitrary and incomplete, and altogether inadequate for the specialist, who must henceforth depend upon the manuscripts.

As far as European shawl history is concerned, J. Rey, *Études pour servir a l'histoire des châles* (Paris, 1823), is of fundamental importance, though concerned primarily with the French industry in its early years. The Edinburgh shawl industry has not hitherto been written about, and very little literature exists on the Norwich shawl, apart from what can be gleaned from the various gazetteers, trade directories, and House of Commons Reports of the early nineteenth century. The Paisley shawl industry, on the other hand, is the subject of several useful monographs. The best and most authoritative is Matthew Blair, *The Paisley Shawl* (Paisley, 1904), which should be read in conjunction with A. M. Stewart, *The History and Romance of the Paisley Shawl* (Paisley, 1946). The latter is full of inaccuracies but is nevertheless valuable for its human approach and conveys the spirit of the Paisley weaving tradition better than any other work. Other original but shorter contributions to the subject are W. Cross, *Changes in the style of Paisley Shawls* (Paisley, 1872), which is useful but not always reliable; an anonymous article entitled *The imitation shawl trade*, which appeared in the *Paisley Herald*, 12th November, 1859; and another anonymous article, *Paisley—the shawl trade*, which appeared in *Hogg's Weekly Instructor*, Edinburgh, 28th November, 1846.

Finally, special mention must be made of the sample books at the Patent Office, London, where many original shawl patterns, with their dates, are registered. Unfortunately, these are not easily accessible, and facilities for study are necessarily dependent upon securing special concessions from the Comptroller-General of Patents.

MANUSCRIPTS AND OTHER ARCHIVAL
SOURCE MATERIAL

BRITISH MUSEUM

ANONYMOUS. *The Costume of the Persians.* Compiled in the late seventeenth century. Add. MSS. 5254.

CASTLE MUSEUM, NORWICH

Correspondence (in MSS) exchanged between Norwich residents and Mr Sydney Vacher on the history of the local shawl trade, dated 1897.

INDIA OFFICE LIBRARY AND ARCHIVES (Commonwealth Relations Office, London, S.W.1).

ANONYMOUS. *A Journey into Cashmere (in 1846)*, Elliot Papers, MSS. Eur. F.58.

EAST INDIA COMPANY. *The Letter Books*, containing copies of despatches from the Directors of the Company to their servants in India and elsewhere.

Home Miscellaneous Volumes, containing original papers exchanged between London and the Company's stations in the East.

MOORCROFT, WILLIAM. *Notice of particulars respecting the manufacture of shawls in Kashmeer*, dated 25th April, 1821. 23 pages. MSS. Eur. D.260.

Shawl manufacture. Dated 1823. 97 pages. MSS. Eur. D.264.

Shawl manufacture. Dated 1823. (A slightly revised version of the preceding MS., addressed to 'The Hon'ble Court of Directors [of the East India Company].' 49 pages. MSS. Eur. E.113.

Letters to C. T. Metcalfe. Written between 1812 and 1820. MSS. Eur. F.38.

'*Book containing illustrations of the various trades in Kashmir with their respective implements and the corresponding accounts of processes of manufacture.*' MS. volume with 86 original paintings by a native artist, with commentary in Persian. The title is written in handwriting identical to that of Moorcroft, and I have therefore assumed it to have once formed part of the Moorcroft manuscripts. Oriental Volume No. 71.

PAISLEY MUSEUM AND ART GALLERY

Letters and other papers relating to the evidence given to the Conseil Supérieur du Commerce, Paris, by a delegation of Paisley manufacturers in July, 1860.

PATENT OFFICE, LONDON

Sample shawl fabrics, registered in Class VIII, Books I to X, dating from 1839 onwards.

CATALOGUES

DELHI EXHIBITION, 1902–3. Official catalogue, entitled *Indian Art at Delhi*, compiled by Sir George Watt. Calcutta, 1903.

GREAT EXHIBITION OF 1851. *Illustrated Catalogue*, published by the Art Journal, 1851.

MORRISON, McCHLERY & Co., Auctioneers, Glasgow. *Catalogue of Paisley shawls from private collections, sold at the North Gallery, Crown Halls, Glasgow, 2nd December, 1942.* *Catalogue of Paisley shawls from private collections, sold at the North Gallery, Crown Halls, Glasgow, 17th February, 1943.*

Catalogue of Paisley Shawls from private collections, sold at the North Gallery, Crown Halls, Glasgow, 6th December, 1943.

PAISLEY FREE PUBLIC LIBRARY AND MUSEUM. *Catalogue of Special Loan Exhibition of Paisley Shawls and similar fabrics.* Paisley, 1900.

PARIS UNIVERSAL EXHIBITION OF 1867. *Catalogue of the British Section.* London, 1868.

UNIVERSITY OF LEEDS. *Catalogue of Embroidered and woven Indian shawls and historic textiles from the Victoria and Albert Museum. Exhibited in the Department of Textile Industries, 1st–15th May, 1920.*

GENERAL WORKS

* An asterisk marks those works available at the
Library of the Victoria and Albert Museum

★AĪN-I-AKBARĪ. (The Institutes of Akbar), compiled by Abul Fazl 'Allami. Edited in the original Persian by H. Blochmann, 2 vols., Calcutta, 1872. Translated in 3 vols. by H. Blochmann and Col. H. S. Jarrett. Calcutta, 1891–4.

★ANONYMOUS. *Kashmeer and its Shawls.* London, 1875.

ANONYMOUS. *New evidence for the study of Kashmir textile history.* Journal of Indian Textile History, Ahmedabad, No. 1, 1955.

ANONYMOUS. *Paisley—The Shawl trade.* Hogg's Weekly Instructor, Edinburgh, 28th November, 1846, pp. 215–18.

★BADEN POWELL, B. H. *Handbook of the Manufactures and Arts of the Punjab,* forming vol. II to the *Handbook of the Economic Products of the Punjab.* Lahore, 1872.

BAIRD THOMAS. *General view of the County of Middlesex.* Board of Agriculture, London, 1793.

BAKEWELL, ROBERT. *Observations on the influence of soil and climate upon wool.* Board of Agriculture, London, 1808.

BARKER, A. F. *The textile industries of Kashmir.* Indian Textile Journal, Vol. XLIII, No. 508, 1933.

BATES, C. E. *A Gazetteer of Kashmir and the adjacent Districts.* Calcutta, 1873.

★BERNIER, FRANÇOIS. *Travels in the Mogul Empire, 1656–68,* revised translation by A. Constable. London, 1891.

★BLAIR, MATTHEW. *The Paisley Shawl and the men who produced it.* Paisley, 1904.

★BLAKELY, EDWARD, T. *History of the manufactures of Norwich.* Norwich, n.d. (c. 1850).

★BLYTH, G. K. *The Norwich Guide.* Norwich, 1842.

BOGLE, GEORGE. *Narratives of the Mission of George Bogle to Tibet (1774),* edited by C. R. Markham. London, 1876.

★CROSS, WILLIAM. *Descriptive Sketch of changes in the style of Paisley Shawls.* The text of a lecture delivered in January, 1872, reprinted from *The Paisley and Renfrewshire Gazette.*

Cyclopaedia of India and of Eastern and Southern Asia, edited by E. Balfour, 2nd edn., 5 vols. Madras, 1871.

DUBEUX, LOUIS. *La Perse.* Paris, 1841.

★FALKE, OTTO VON. *Decorative Silks.* 1936, fig. 35.

★FISCHEL, O., AND BOEHN, MAX VON. *Modes and manners of the nineteenth century,* translated from the German, 4 vols. London, 1927.

FOOT, JESSE. *Life of Hunter.* London, 1794.

★FORBES WATSON, J. *The Textiles Manufactures and the costume of the people of India.* London, 1867.

★FORSTER, GEORGE. *Journey from Bengal to England,* 2 vols. London, 1798.

FRYER, JOHN. *A new account of the East Indies and Persia,* 3 vols. Hakluyt Society, 1909–16.

★*General History of the County of Norfolk.* Printed by John Stacy. Norwich, 1829.

GILMOUR, DAVID. *Gordon's Loan sixty-odd years ago.* Privately printed. Paisley, 1891.

★GRAND-CARTERET, J. *Des Elégances de la Toilette.* Paris, 1911.

GRIER, S. C. *Letters of Warren Hastings to his wife.* London, 1905.

HÜGEL, BARON CHARLES. *Travels in Kashmir and the Punjab.* London, 1845.

JOHNSTONE, D. C. *The woollen manufactures of the Punjab.* Lahore, 1885.

★*Household Words.* A weekly journal, conducted by Charles Dickens, London, 1850–9.

★*Illustrated Catalogue of the Great Exhibition, 1851.* Published by the Art Journal, London.

JACQUEMONT, VICTOR. *Voyage dans l'Inde*, 4 vols. Paris, 1841.

JONES, SIR WILLIAM. *Life, writings and correspondence of Sir William Jones* (edited by Lord Teignmouth). London, 1807.

*KING, M. R. *Cashmere Shawls*. Cincinnati Museum, Review No. 5, 1921.

*LAPAUZE, H. *Ingres, sa vie et son oeuvre*. Paris, 1911.

LAWRENCE, WALTER R. *The Valley of Kashmir*. London, 1895.

LEGOUX DE FLAIX. *Essai historique, geographique et politique sur l'Indoustan*, 2 vols. Paris, 1807.

*LOMULLER, L. *Existe-t-il des châles Ternaux dessinés par Isabey?* Beaux Arts, Paris, No. 120, 15th April, 1949.

McCULLOCH, J. R. *A statistical account of the British Empire*, 2nd edn., 2 vols. London, 1839.

MANRIQUE, SEBASTIEN. *The Travels of Sebastien Manrique, 1629–43*. Hakluyt Society, 2 vols., 1926–7.

MANUCCI, NICCOLAO. *Storia do Mogor or Mogul India, 1653–1708*. Translated by William Irvine, 4 vols., London, 1906.

MAZE-SENCIER, ALPHONSE. *Les Fournisseurs de Napoléon Ier et des deux Impératrices*, Paris, 1893.

Memorial of the Operative Weavers in Paisley to the Sheriff Depute of Refrewshire, presented 12th December, 1812. (A copy is preserved in Paisley Public Library).

MERRIMAN, J. J. *John Hunter at Earl's Court, 1764–93*. Privately printed, London, 1886.

MOORCROFT, W. (AND TREBECK, G.). *Travels in the Himalayan Provinces of Hindustan and the Punjab: in Ladakh and Kashmir, 1919–25*, 2 vols., edited by H. H. Wilson. London, 1841. (*For Moorcroft's unpublished MSS. see under MANUSCRIPTS.*)

*MURPHY, J. *A Treatise on the Art of Weaving*, 2nd edn. (revised and enlarged). Glasgow, 1827.

New Statistical Account of Scotland, 15 vols., 1845 (the chapter on Paisley was written in 1837).

PELSAERT, FRANCISCO. *Remonstrantie*, translated by W. H. Moreland and P. Geyl as *Jahangir's India*. London, 1925.

RACINET, AUGUSTE. *La Costume historique*, 6 vols., Paris, 1888.

RÉMUSAT, MADAME DE. *Memoirs*, translated by Mrs Cashel Hoey and Mr J. Lillie. London, 1880.

Reports from Assistant Handloom Weaver's Commissioners, 1839–40. Printed by order of the House of Commons, in 3 vols. (5 parts), 1939–40.

*REY, J. *Études pour servir a l'Histoire des Châles*. Paris, 1823.

ROE, SIR THOMAS. *The Embassy of Sir Thomas Roe to the Court of the Great Mogul, 1615–19*, edited by W. Foster. Hakluyt Society, 1899.

*RUDD, W. R. *Norwich Master Weavers*. Proceedings of the Norwich Gossip Club, 1910–11.

*SIMPSON, WILLIAM. *India, Ancient and Modern: a series of illustrations of the country and people . . . Executed in chromo-lithographs from Drawings by W.S., with descriptive literature by John William Kaye*. London, 1867.

SOUTHEY, THOMAS. *The rise, progess and present state of Colonial wools*. London, 1848.

Statistical Account of Scotland: from communications of ministers of the different parishes, compiled by Sir John Sinclair, 21 vols., 1791–9.

STEINBACH, LT.-COL. *The Punjab*. London, 1845.

*STEWART, A. M. *The history and romance of the Paisley Shawl*. Paisley, 1946.

TESSIER, M. *Mémoire sur l'Importation en France des Chevres à duvet de Cachemire*. A reprint of a paper read at l'Academie Royale des Sciences (Paris), 13th September, 1819.

THÉVENOT, JEAN DE. *Troisieme partie des Voyages de, contenant la Relation de l'Hindostan, des Nouveaux Mogols, et des autres Peuples et Pays des Indes*. Paris, 1684.

THORNTON, EDWARD. *A gazetteer of the countries adjacent to India*, 2 vols. London, 1844.

THORP, ROBERT. *Cashmere misgovernment.* London, 1870.

TORRENS, LT.-COL. *Travels in Ladak, Tartary, and Kashmir.* London, 1863.

TURNER, CAPTAIN SAMUEL *An account of an embassy to the court of the Teshoo Lama, in Tibet (1783).* London, 1806.

VALLE, PIETRO DELLA. *The Travels of Pietro della Valle.* Hakluyt Society, 2 vols., 1891.

VIGNE, G. T. *Travels in Kashmir.* London, 1842.

★WARNER, SIR FRANK. *The Silk Industry of the United Kingdom: its origin and development.* London, 1921.

★WATT, SIR GEORGE. *Indian art at Delhi, being the official catalogue of the Delhi Exhibition, 1902–3.* Calcutta, 1903.

★WEIBEL, A. C. *Two thousand years of textiles.* Detroit Institute of Arts, Detroit, 1952.

WHYTE, DOROTHY. *The Paisley Shawl.* Scottish Woollens, No. 39, June, 1949 (4 pages, 7 plates, including some in colour).

WILSON, H. H. Compiler and editor of Moorcroft's posthumous *Travels* (s.v. Moorcroft, William).

WILSON, JOHN. *General view of the agriculture of Renfrewshire.* Board of Agriculture, London, 1812.

CATALOGUE

WHEREVER possible colours have been identified from the first edition of the *British Colour Council Dictionary of Colour Standards* (published in 1934 by the British Colour Council, 13 Portman Square, London, W.1), and the actual chart numbers have been quoted. These identifications relate to the condition of the material when examined, no allowances having been made for dirtiness or fading.

The analyses of fabrics were made by Mr R. J. Varney, Assistant in the Indian Section, Victoria and Albert Museum, who was also responsible for other help in connection with the preparation of the catalogue. Where doubt was felt about analyses, samples were sent to the Director of the Shirley Institute, Manchester, for independent opinion.

FRONTISPIECE. FRAGMENT OF SHAWL-CLOTH: loom-woven, Kashmir, 18th century.
Warp and weft: goat-fleece.
Weave: 2×2 twill, with 88 warps to the inch.
Size: H. 1 ft. 10 in. W. 8½ in.
Collection: Calico Museum of Textiles, Ahmedabad. Inv. No. C.14–S.14.

PLATE 1. FRAGMENT OF SHAWL BORDER: loom-woven, Kashmir, 17th century.
Warp and weft: goat-fleece.
Weave: 2×2 twill, with 96 warps to the inch.
Size: W. 14½ in. H. 5¾ in.
Colours: mistletoe, victrix blue, sky green, (dark) beryl blue, cherry, on a banana ground. B.C.C. Nos. 9, 47, 101, 117, 185 and 64.
Collection: Calico Museum of Textiles, Ahmedabad.
Remarks: This fragment is probably part of the shawl illustrated in the catalogue of the *Loan Exhibition of Antiquities*, Coronation Durbar, Delhi, 1911, p. 35, plate xv (d). There it was described as having been 'conferred as a *khil'at* by one of the late Moghul Emperors on a Chief of Bikaner'. Another, smaller fragment of the same shawl was given by the

Calico Museum of Textiles to the Victoria and Albert Museum (I.S. 70–1954).

PLATE 2. SHAWL FRAGMENT: loom-woven, Kashmir, early 18th century.
Warp and weft: goat-fleece.
Weave: 2×2 twill, with 92 warps to the inch.
Size: H. 11 in. W. 4½ in. Height of floral motif, 7¾ in.
Colours: maize, cyclamen, pink, neyron rose, claret, victrix blue, straw, Cambridge blue, powder blue, and white, on a banana ground. B.C.C. Nos. 5, 33, 35, 36, 47, 51, 191, 193, 1, and 64.
Collection: Victoria and Albert Museum (given by Mr N. H. Heeramaneck in 1924). Inv. No. I.M.48–1924, Neg. No. G.587.

PLATE 3. PART OF A SHAWL: loom-woven, Kashmir, first half of the 18th century.
Warp and weft: goat-fleece.
Weave: 2×2 twill, with 68 warps to the inch.
Size: W. 3 ft. 9 in. H. 9½ in. Height of cones, 8 in.
Colours: lichen green, malmaison rose, claret, saxe blue, victrix blue, satinwood, beryl blue, on a maize ground. B.C.C. Nos. 8, 16, 36, 45, 47, 65, 117, and 5.

Collection: Victoria and Albert Museum (bought in 1913). Inv. No. I.M.166–1913. Neg. No. G.586.

PLATES 4 and 5. SHAWL: loom-woven, Kashmir, late 17th or early 18th century.
Warp and weft: goat-fleece.
Weave: 2×2 twill, with 116–120 warps to the inch.
Size: L. 6 ft. 10 in. W. 4 ft. 2 in. Height of cones, 5 in. approx.
Colours: red, yellow, three shades of green, on a cream ground.
Collection: Museum of Fine Art, Boston, Mass., Inv. No. 45.540.

PLATE 6. SHAWL FRAGMENT: loom-woven, Kashmir, mid-18th century.
Warp and weft: goat-fleece.
Weave: 2×2 twill, with 94 warps to the inch.
Size: H. 12 in. W. 8½ in. Height of cones, 8¾ in.
Colours: blossom pink, claret, straw, midnight, Cambridge blue, juniper, on a banana ground. B.C.C. Nos. 34, 36, 51, 90, 191, 192, and 64.
Collection: Victoria and Albert Museum (bought in 1913). Inv. No. I.M.169–1913, Neg. No. G.587.

PLATE 7. PART OF A SHAWL: loom-woven, Kashmir, first half of the 18th century.
Warp and weft: goat-fleece.
Weave: 2×2 twill, with 88 warps to the inch.
Size: W. 2 ft. H. 9¾ in. Height of cones 7¾ in.
Colours: champagne, blossom pink, peony red, saxe blue, victrix blue, beryl blue, on a cream ground. B.C.C. Nos. 4, 34, 37, 45, 47, 117, and 3.
Collection: Victoria and Albert Museum (bought in 1913). Inv. No. I.M.165–1913, Neg. No. G.587.

PLATE 8. PART OF A SHAWL: loom-woven, Kashmir, second half of the 18th century.
Warp and weft: goat-fleece.
Weave: 2×2 twill, with 94 warps to the inch.
Size: W. 3 ft. 11½ in. H. 11 in. Height of cones, 7¼ in.
Colours: champagne, maize, cyclamen pink, claret, forget-me-not, midnight, beryl blue, delphinium, on a cream ground. B.C.C. Nos. 4, 5, 33, 36, 84, 90, 117, 195, and 3
Collection: Victoria and Albert Museum (bought in 1913). Inv. No. I.M.302–1913, Neg. No. G.589.

PLATE 9. PART OF A SHAWL: loom-woven, Kashmir, second half of the 18th century.
Warp and weft: goat-fleece.
Weave: 2×2 twill, with 72 warps to the inch.
Size: L. 9 ft. 4 in. W. 4 ft. 4 in. Height of cones, 8 in.
Colours: cyclamen pink, claret, victrix blue, banana, satinwood, delphinium, on a white ground. B.C.C. Nos. 33, 36, 47, 64, 65, 195, and 1.
Collection: Victoria and Albert Museum (given by Miss M. Davis in 1915). Inv. No. I.M.17–1915, Neg. No. G.588.

PLATE 10. FRAGMENT OF CLOTH (A SLEEVE): loom-woven, probably Persian, 18th century.
Warp and weft: goat-fleece.
Weave: 2×1 twill, with 128 warps to the inch.
Size: H. 2 ft. 2 in. W. 9 in.
Colours: Tyrian rose, light jasper red, Nopal red, spectrum red, flame scarlet, ox-blood red, orange, olive yellow, myrtle green, duck green, dark green, lettuce green, Orient blue and pale Glaucus blue, on an ivory yellow ground. (In this case the colour-standard is Robert Ridgway, *Colour standards*, Washington, D.C., 1912.)
Collection: The Detroit Institute of Arts, Detroit.
Remarks: I have unfortunately not been able to examine this interesting fabric at first hand, but the unfamiliarity of certain features raises doubts about the Kashmir attribution traditionally given to it. For instance, the twill is 2×1 instead of the usual 2×2; and the floral pattern, based on contemporary Coromandel chintz, has no Kashmir parallel. Sample fibres kindly supplied by Mrs A. C. Weibel were sent for analysis to the Wool Industries Research Association, Leeds, and it was reported that they were closer to Kirman (Persian) goat-fleece than that ordinarily used in Kashmir.

PLATE 11. PART OF A SHAWL: loom-woven, Kashmir, second half of the 18th century.
Warp and weft: goat-fleece.
Weave: 2×2 twill, with 96 warps to the inch.
Size: W. 2 ft. 3 in. H. 1 ft. 2 in. Height of cones 11½ in.
Colours: neyron rose, claret, victrix blue, banana, falcon, calamine blue, on a pale khaki ground. B.C.C. Nos. 35, 36, 47, 64, 130, 163, and 72.
Collection: Victoria and Albert Museum (bought in 1913). Inv. No. I.M.164–1913, Neg. No. G.591.

PLATE 12. PART OF A SHAWL: loom-woven, Kashmir, late 18th or early 19th century.
Warp and weft: goat-fleece.
Weave: 2×2 twill, with 54 warps to the inch.
Size: L. 2 ft. 6 in. W. 1 ft. 9 in.
Colours: red, pink, yellow, green a shade of blue, on a blue ground.
Collection: Museum of Fine Art, Boston, Mass. Inv. No. 99, 163, Neg. No. 1732.

PLATE 13. SHAWL: loom-woven, Kashmir, late 18th or early 19th century.
Warp and weft: goat-fleece.
Weave: 2×2 twill, with 76 warps to the inch.
Size: L. 9 ft. 7 in. W. 2 ft. 7 in.
Colours: warps are a dull green-blue; weft colours form varicoloured square backgrounds for flowers. Three reds, two pinks, three oranges, three yellows, five shades of green, two shades of green-blue, four blues, a violet and a cream.
Collection: Museum of Fine Art, Boston, Mass. Inv. No. 00.582.

PLATES 14 and 15. SHAWL: loom-woven, Kashmir, early 19th century.
Warp and weft: goat-fleece.
Weave: 2×2 twill, with 66 warps to the inch on the centre piece, and 130 warps to the inch on applied border.
Size: 5 ft. 11 in. by 5 ft. 11 in.
Colours: red, pink, three blues, green, yellow, on a cream ground.
Collection: Museum of Fine Art, Boston, Mass. Inv. No. 21.1333, Neg. No. 14679.

PLATE 16. SHAWL: loom-woven, Kashmir, c. 1800.
Warp and weft: goat-fleece.
Weave: 2×2 twill, with 100 and 80 warps to the inch.
Size: L. 13 ft. 4 in. W. 4 ft. 7 in. Height of floral motif, 11½ in.
Colours: Main ground, Brunswick green.
Wide border, victrix blue, coral, bunting yellow, raspberry, white, on a bunting azure ground.
Narrow border, victrix blue, Brunswick green, bunting yellow, raspberry, on a white ground. B.C.C. Nos. M.grd., 104. W.brdr., 47, 93, 113, 116, 159, 1, and 131. N.brdr., 47, 104, 113, 159, and 1.
Collection: Calico Museum of Textiles, Ahmedabad. Ref. No. 276.

PLATE 17. SHAWL: loom-woven, Kashmir, c. 1800.
Warp and weft: goat-fleece.
Weave: 2×2 twill, with 90 warps to the inch.
Size: L. 10 ft. 5 in. W. 4 ft. 6 in.
Colours: cyclamen pink, peony red, victrix blue, saffron, stone white, cedar green, delphinium, on a moss green ground. B.C.C. Nos. 33, 37, 47, 54, 61, 80, 195 and 174.
Collection: Property of the Countess of Powis.
Remarks: This shawl is claimed on hearsay evidence to have been brought from India by the 2nd Lord Clive, about 1804.

PLATE 18. SCARF OR GIRDLE: loom-woven, Kashmir, early 19th century.
Warp and weft: goat-fleece (the edgings reinforced with silk warps).
Weave: 2×2 twill, with 96 warps to the inch. End borders separately woven.
Size: L. 9 ft. 4 in. W. 1 ft. 1 in.
Colours: maize, mistletoe, malmaison rose, claret, victrix blue, bunting azure, on a cream ground. B.C.C. Nos. 5, 9, 16, 36, 47, 131, and 3.
Collection: Victoria and Albert Museum (given by the National Art Collections Fund in 1950). Inv. No. I.S.177–1950, Neg. No. M.285.

PLATE 19. PART OF A SHAWL: loom-woven, Kashmir, early 19th century.
Warp and weft: goat-fleece.
Weave: 2×2 twill, with 90 warps to the inch.
Size: L. 4 ft. 1 in. W. 1 ft. 3 in.
Colours: A ground pattern of claret, saxe blue, straw, geranium pink, juniper, and jet black; plus in the border, cream, Indian yellow, and cardinal. B.C.C. Nos. 36, 45, 184, 192, 220, plus 3, 6, and 186.
Collection: Royal Scottish Museum, Edinburgh. Inv. No. 1920–393.

PLATE 20. PART OF A SHAWL: loom-woven, Kashmir, c. 1820.
Warp and weft: goat-fleece.
Weave: 2×2 twill, with 75 warps to the inch.
Size: L. 2 ft. 5 in. W. 1 ft. 9 in. Height of large cones, 1 ft. 3 in. Depth of lead, 1 ft. 3½ in.
Colours: ivory, maize, lichen green, nigger brown, peony red, indigo, forget-me-not, orchid pink, cypress green, beetroot. B.C.C. Nos. 2, 5, 8, 20, 37, 48, 84, 106, 175, 200.
Collection: Victoria and Albert Museum (bought in 1883). Inv. No. 1573–1883 I.S., Neg. No. G.323.

PLATE 21. SHAWL FRAGMENT: loom-woven, Kashmir, c. 1820.
Warp and weft: goat-fleece.
Weave: 2×2 twill, with 86 warps to the inch.
Size: L. 1 ft. 11½ in. W. 1 ft. 8½ in. Height of cones, 1 ft. 1 in.
Colours: maize, eau-de-nil, cyclamen pink, peony, indigo, ecru, calamine blue, with peony warp threads. B.C.C. Nos. 5, 21, 33, 37, 48, 63, 163, plus 37 (warp threads).
Collection: Victoria and Albert Museum (bought in 1883). Inv. No. 2090–1883 I.S., Neg. No. G.324.

PLATE 22. SCARF OR GIRDLE: embroidered with the needle, Kashmir, c. 1830.
Worked with silks on a ground of goat-fleece, the latter of 2×2 twill, with 100 warps to the inch. The embroidery in stem, satin and darning stitches.
Size: L. 8 ft. 4 in. W. 2 ft. 4½ in.
Colours: The centre field is cardinal red (B.C.C. No. 186). The embroidery is blos-

som pink, victrix blue, satinwood, salmon, bunting azure, nutria, juniper, jet black, and stone white, on a peony red ground. B.C.C. Nos. 34, 47, 65, 91, 131, 139, 192, 220, 61, and 37.
Collection: Victoria and Albert Museum (given by Mrs Marian Lewis in 1907). Inv. No. 501–1907, Neg. No. 57659.

PLATE 23. SCARF OR GIRDLE: loom-woven, Kashmir, embroidered in stem, satin and darning stitches with wool, illustrating stories from Nizami's *Khamsa*, c. 1840.
Warp and weft: goat-fleece.
Weave: 1×1 twill, with 2×2 twill strip at each end. 70 warps to the inch.
Size: L. 4 ft. 11 in. W. 1 ft. 6 in.
Colours: neyron rose, rose pink, cyclamen pink, beryl blue, bunting azure, cherry, juniper, stone white on a jet black ground. B.C.C. Nos. 35, 52, 53, 117, 131, 185, 192, 61, and 220.
Collection: Victoria and Albert Museum (transferred from the India Office in 1879), Inv. No. 803 I.S., Neg. No. 57660.

PLATE 24. GIRDLE OR SCARF: embroidered with the needle, probably worked by Kashmiri emigrant in the Punjab, second half of the 19th century.
Worked with silks on a plain muslin ground of 66 warps to the inch. The embroidery is inlaid oriental stitch and stem stitch.
Size: L. 4 ft. 9 in. W. 1 ft. Height of sprays, 5 in.
Colours: maize, almond green, blossom pink, saffron, water green, bunting azure, cherry, jet black, on a stone white ground. B.C.C. Nos. 5, 10, 34, 54, 99, 131, 185, 220 and 61.
Collection: Victoria and Albert Museum (given by Miss M. K. Lawrence in 1920). Ref. No. I.M.212–1920, Neg. No. 57661.
Remarks: This piece has unusual features, including the use of muslin for the ground. The style, however, has points of similarity with other Kashmir shawls of the period (cf. Plate 33, especially the treatment of the cones in the corner of the field).

PLATE 25. PART OF A SHAWL: loom-woven, Kashmir, *c.* 1820.
Warp and weft: goat-fleece.
Weave: 2×2 twill, with 72 warps to the inch.
Size: L. 2 ft. 5½ in. W. 1 ft. 7½ in. Height of large cones, 10⅜ in. Height of small cones, 4 in.
Colours: mistletoe, peony red, straw, chartreuse yellow (nrst.), midnight, falcon, old rose, sky blue, delphinium, ecru on a ruby ground. B.C.C. Nos. 9, 37, 51, 75, 90, 130, 157, 162, 196, 63 and 38.
Collection: Victoria and Albert Museum. No Inv. No., Neg. No. G.595.

PLATE 26. PART OF A SHAWL: loom-woven, Kashmir, *c.* 1820.
Warp and weft: goat-fleece.
Weave: 2×2 twill, with 64 warps to the inch.
Size: L. 2 ft. 2 in. W. 2 ft. 2 in. Height of cones, 7 in.
Colours: mistletoe, nigger brown, victrix blue, straw, strawberry pink, larkspur on a peony red ground. Main ground, claret. B.C.C. Nos. 9, 20, 47, 51, 182, 196 and 37. Main ground, 36.
Collection: Victoria and Albert Museum (bought in 1883). Inv. No. 1359b–1883 I.S., Neg. No. G.598.

PLATE 27. PART OF A SHAWL: loom-woven, Kashmir, *c.* 1830.
Warp and weft: goat-fleece.
Weave: 2×2 twill, with 72 warps to the inch.
Size: L. 3 ft. 6 in. W. 1 ft. 7 in. Height of large cones, 11 in.
Colours: champagne, ecru, midnight, bunting azure, old rose, raspberry, garnet on a garnet warp; plus in narrow border: Cambridge blue and delphinium on a cream ground. B.C.C. Nos. 4, 63, 131, 157, 159, and 160 plus 191, 195, and 3.
Collection: Victoria and Albert Museum (bought in 1883), Inv. No. 2084a–1883, Neg. No. G.320.

PLATE 28. PART OF A SHAWL: loom-woven, Kashmir, *c.* 1825.
Warp and weft: goat-fleece.
Weave: 2×2 twill, with 75 warps to the inch.

Size: L. 2 ft. 5 in. W. 1 ft. 5 in. Height of large cones, 10¼ in. Depth of lead, 10½ in.
Colours: blossom pink, peony red, spectrum blue, turquoise green, apricot, garnet, jet black, on a cream ground. B.C.C. Nos. 34, 37, 86, 121, 143, 160, 220 and 3.
Collection: Victoria and Albert Museum (bought in 1883). Inv. No. 2081a–1883 I.S., Neg. No. M.705.

PLATE 29. PART OF A SHAWL: loom-woven, Kashmir, *c.* 1830.
Warp and weft: goat-fleece.
Weave: 2×2 twill, with 94 warps to the inch.
Size: L 4 ft. 4 in. W. 2 ft. 6 in.
Colours: nigger brown, claret, peony red, lemon, garnet, cypress green, juniper, delphinium, on a cream ground. B.C.C. Nos. 20, 36, 37, 52, 160, 175, 192, 195 and 3.
Collection: Victoria and Albert Museum (bought in 1883). Inv. No. 1685–1883 I.S., Neg. No. G.321.

PLATE 30. SHAWL: loom-woven, Kashmir, *c.* 1830.
Warp and weft: goat-fleece.
Weave: 2×2 twill, with:
84 warps to the inch.
60 „ „ „ white ground.
110 „ „ „ narrow border.
Size: L. 9 ft. 8 in. W. 4 ft. 7 in. Height of cones, 1 ft. 1½ in.
Colours: cream, Indian yellow, claret, peony red, straw, midnight, old rose, sky blue, Cambridge blue, juniper, delphinium, jet black on a cream *centre* ground. B.C.C. Nos. 3, 6, 36, 37, 51, 90, 157, 162, 191, 192, 195, 220 with 3 (centre ground).
Collection: Victoria and Albert Museum (bought in 1883). Inv. No. 2000–1883 I.S., Neg. No. M.1556. Colour slide No. 46688.

PLATE 31. SHAWL: loom-woven, Kashmir, early 19th century.
Warp and weft: goat-fleece.
Weave: 2×2 twill, with 82 warps to the inch.
Size: L. 9 ft. 11 in. W. 4 ft. 1 in. Five rows of cones, height of each cone, 2½ in.
Colours: blossom pink, claret, straw (traces),

beryl blue, nutria, geranium pink, delphinium (two shades), jet black (darns), on a champagne ground. B.C.C. Nos. 34, 36, 51, 117, 139, 184, 195, 220 and 4.

Note—In almost every case the brown thread (nutria), has been replaced with black darning.

Collection: Victoria and Albert Museum (bequeathed by Sir Michael Sadler in 1948). Inv. No. I.S.95–1948, Neg. No. M.649.

Remarks: Shawls with designs of this type were made without interruption from the late 18th century until the mid-19th. For an example illustrated in a Rajput miniature dated 1795, see H. Goetz, *Jahrbuch der Asiatische Kunst*, vol. I, plate 39.

PLATE 32. SHAWL: loom-woven, Kashmir, *c*. 1830.

Warp and weft: goat-fleece.

Weave: 2×2 twill, with 86 warps to the inch.

Size: L. 12 ft. 3 in. W. 4 ft. 2 in. Height of large cones, 10½ in. Height of small cones on ground, 2½ in.

Colours: maize, cyclamen pink, peony red, midnight, beryl blue, delphinium, beetroot, jet black, on a cream ground. B.C.C. Nos. 5, 33, 37, 90, 117, 195, 200, 220 and 3.

Collection: Victoria and Albert Museum (bequeathed by Sir Michael Sadler in 1948). Inv. No. I.S.96–1948, Neg. No. G.332.

PLATE 33. REVERSIBLE SCARF: loom-wove, some pattern-outlines needle embroidered, Kashmir, 1865.

Warp and weft: goat-fleece.

Weave: 2×2 twill, with 100 warps to the inch in the main pattern and 92 warps to the inch in the border.

Size: L. 8 ft. 4 in. W. 1 ft. 5 in.

Colours: malachite green, ruby, saffron, marigold, amaranth pink, beryl blue, garter blue, pansy, cardinal, jet black, cream on a cream ground. B.C.C. Nos. 23, 38, 54, 56, 107, 117, 132, 180, 186, 220, and 3.

Collection: Victoria and Albert Museum (transferred from the India Office in 1879), Inv. No. 0804 I.S., Neg. No. M.284.

Note—Attached to this scarf is a label which reads: 'Scarf of quite new fabric. Shows the same on both sides. Locality: Kashmir. Exhibitor: Dewān Kirpa Rām. Price £37 12 0.' Catalogue of the British Section, Paris Univ. Exhibition of 1867. London, 1868. Group IV, Class XXXII, No. 12 (p. 289).

PLATE 34. MAN'S OVERCOAT: made up from Kashmir shawl-cloth, loom-woven, early 19th century.

Warp and weft: goat-fleece.

Weave: 2×2 twill, with 80 warps to the inch.

Size: L 4 ft. W. (across sleeves) 5 ft. 2 in.

Colours: maize, malmaison rose, claret, saxe blue, victrix blue, geranium pink, Cambridge blue on a cream ground. B.C.C. Nos. 5, 16, 36, 45, 47, 184, 191 and 3.

Collection: Victoria and Albert Museum (bought in 1928). Inv. No. I.M.32–1928, Neg. No. G.1026.

PLATE 35. SHAWL: loom-woven, Kashmir, *c*. 1870.

Warp and weft: goat-fleece.

Weave: 2×2 twill, with 82 warps to the inch.

Size: L. 10 ft. 6 in. W. 4 ft. 11½ in.

Colours: cream, Indian yellow, malachite green, petunia, peacock blue, jet black, on a Union Jack Red ground. B.C.C. Nos. 3, 6, 23, 108, 120, 220, and 210.

Collection: Property of Mrs MacCormack, 23 Courtfield Gardens, London, S.W.5.

PLATE 36. SHAWL: embroidered with the needle, probably Persian, mid-19th century. Worked with silks on a ground of goat-fleece, the latter of 2×1 twill with 98 warps to the inch. The stitches are mainly darning- and shading-stitch, the edging being in cord- and back-stitch. The applied fringe is apparently of European origin. The shawl has four inscriptions embroidered in Persian characters which have been translated as follows:

O, Almighty Protector! Blessing to us (?)!
Trust of S . . .

★　　　★　　　★　　　★

On your stature, (this) sheet, O Silver-bodied
Is like the Cypress tree as it graces the garden!

★　　　★　　　★　　　★

Original commission.
New design, new exposition, distinguished.

( ) *plant*, ( ) *embroidered.*
A bouquet of European (Frank) plants,
Rosebud with curved edges.
Keeper of the Moon! Maker of Fine Embroidery!
Excellent! Excellent!

     ✻   ✻   ✻   ✻

First . . .

Colours: cyclamen pink, neyron rose, victrix blue, straw, ecru, falcon, bunting azure, juniper, on a cream ground. B.C.C. Nos. 33, 35, 47, 51, 63, 130, 131, 192 and 3.
Collection: Victoria and Albert Museum, Ref. No. I.S.1–1949, Neg. No. L.1568.
Remarks: This unusual piece has several features which would be difficult to associate with a shawl of Kashmir origin. For instance, the drawing shows blend of naturalism and stylization unusual for a late shawl; colours are slightly unfamiliar, and the ground weave is 2×1 twill instead of the usual 2×2.

PLATE 37. SHAWL: loom-woven, Norwich, *c.* 1835.
Warp and weft: silk warp and cotton weft.
Weave: 3×1 warp twill, with 84 warps to the inch.
Size: L. 8 ft. 1 in. W. 3 ft. 9½ in. Height of cones, 1 ft. 3 in.
Colours: saxe blue, victrix blue, lemon, moss green, stone white, on a ground consisting of claret warps and cinnamon wefts. B.C.C. Nos. 45, 47, 52, 174, 61 with 36, and 204.
Collection: Victoria and Albert Museum (bought in 1893), Inv. No. 1155–1893 (T), Neg. No. K.2145.

PLATE 38. SHAWL: loom-woven, Norwich, *c.* 1835.
Warp and weft: silk warp and cotton weft.
Weave: ground 2×2 warp twill, pattern 3×1 warp twill. 84 warps to the inch.
Size: L. 8 ft. 4 in. W. 3 ft. 8 in. Height of cones, 1 ft. 1 in.
Colours: neyron rose, lemon, forget-me-not, adonis, falcon, cream on a cypress green ground. B.C.C. Nos. 35, 52, 84, 85, 130, 3, 175.
Collection: Victoria and Albert Museum

(bought in 1893), Inv. No. 1159–1893 (T), Neg. No. K.2154.

PLATE 39. SHAWL: loom-woven, Norwich, *c.* 1835.
Warp and weft: warp, silk, weft, cotton and silk mixture. Cotton warp and weft in narrow border.
Weave: 1×3 warp twill, with 84 warps to the inch.
Colours: satinwood, bronze green, adonis blue, nutria, white on a ground of neyron rose warps and banana wefts. Narrow border, victrix blue, nutmeg, cypress green on a cream ground. B.C.C. Nos. 65, 79, 85, 139, 1 with 35, and 64; 47, 168, 175, and 3.
Collection: Victoria and Albert Museum (bought in 1893), Inv. No. 1160–1893 (T), Neg. No. K.2153.

PLATE 40. SHAWL: loom-woven, Norwich, *c.* 1850.
Warp and weft: silk warp and woollen weft.
Weave: 3×1 twill, with 86 warps to the inch.
Size: L. 9 ft. 8½ in. W. 4 ft. 8 in. Height of cones, 4 in. 4 rows of cones, 18 cones per row.
Colours: rose pink, victrix blue, tangerine, R.A.F. blue-grey, sage green, cherry on a cream ground. B.C.C. Nos. 32, 47, 55, 156, 173, 185, and 3.
Collection: Bridewell Museum, Norwich. Ref. No. 158–937.

PLATE 41. SHAWL: loom-woven, Norwich, *c.* 1830.
Warp and weft: warps of silk, field weft of silk and goat-fleece, border weft of silk. (Analysed at the Shirley Institute, Manchester).
Weave: 2×2 twill (field), 3×1 twill (border), with 84 warps to the inch (field).
      108 ,, ,, ,, (border).
Size: L. 10 ft. W. 5 ft. 7 in. Height of cones, 6½ in. Two rows of cones, with 16 full cones to a row.
Colours: hydrangea pink, rifle green, neyron rose, saxe blue, victrix blue, satinwood, bronze, raspberry, sage green, on a cream

ground. B.C.C. Nos. 12, 35, 45, 47, 65, 116, 159, 173, and 3.
Collection: Victoria and Albert Museum (given by Miss C. J. Sketchley in 1951), Inv. No. T.17–1951, Neg. No. K.2157.

PLATE 42. SHAWL: loom-woven, with applied border, Norwich, *c.* 1830.
Warp and weft: silk warp and wool weft. (Some cotton fibres are included among the warps in the border.)
Weave: 2×2 twill on the ground, 3×1 twill on the pattern. 80 warps to the inch.
Size: L. 5 ft. 2 in. W. 5 ft.
Colours: maize, forget-me-not, nutria, sage green, cream, on a raspberry ground. Border: maize, rifle green, forget-me-not, crushed strawberry, juniper, Post Office red, on a cream ground. B.C.C. Nos. 5, 84, 139, 173, 3 with 159; 5, 27, 84, 158, 192, 209, and 3.
Collection: Paisley Museum. Ref. No. P.138.

PLATE 43. SHAWL: loom-woven, with applied border, Paisley, *c.* 1825.
Warp and weft: field, silk warp and woollen weft. Border, silk warp and woollen weft.
Weave: 3×2 twill, with 112 warps to the inch.
Size: 1 ft. 3¾ in. square.
Colours: mistletoe, blossom pink, victrix blue, lemon, ivory, on a khaki ground. B.C.C. Nos. 9, 34, 47, 52, 2, and 72.
Collection: Paisley Museum. Ref. No. 43h/42.

PLATE 44. SAMPLE SHAWL FRAGMENT: loom-woven, Edinburgh, 1843. Registered at the Patent Office by the firm of David Sime & Son, Edinburgh, in this year.
Warp and weft: silk warp, wool weft in ground. Coloured wefts, mixture of cotton and wool.
Weave: 3×1 twill, with 96 warps to the inch.
Size: L. 1 ft. 4 in. W. 1 ft. 4½ in.
Colours: maize, hydrangea pink, nigger brown (approx.), adonis blue, Brunswick green, Union Jack red, white, on a banana (approx.) ground. B.C.C. Nos. 5, 12, 20, 85, 104, 210, 1, and 64.
Collection: Patent Office Records, London, Class VIII, Book I, Ref. No. 9391. Published by permission of the Comptroller-General of Patents.

PLATE 45. SAMPLE SHAWL FRAGMENT: loom-woven, Norwich, 1843. Registered at the Patent Office by the firm of H. & E. Willet & Son, Norwich, in this year.
Warp and weft: silk warp, woollen ground weft; the pattern wefts of wool and cotton.
Weave: 3×1 twill, with 104 warps to the inch.
Size: L. 1 ft. 9 in. W. 1 ft. 2 in.
Colours: hydrangea pink, lemon, sea green, falcon, delphinium, Union Jack red, white, on a cream ground. B.C.C. Nos. 12, 52, 102, 130, 195, 210, 1, and 3.
Collection: Patent Office Records, London, Class VIII, Book I, Ref. No. 6240. Published by permission of the Comptroller-General of Patents.

PLATES 46 and 48. SHAWL: loom-woven, Paisley, *c.* 1865. This shawl bears an imitation inscription in pseudo-Persian script.
Warp and weft: warps, mixture of fine wool and silk; weft, wool. White border weft is of cotton.
Weave: 3×1 twill, with 102 warps to the inch.
Size: L. 11 ft. W. 5 ft. 3 in.
Colours: malmaison rose, saffron (approx.), Cossack green, bunting azure, cardinal, stone white, jet black with cardinal warp threads. B.C.C. Nos. 16, 54, 105, 131, 186, 61, and 220; warps, 186.
Collection: Victoria and Albert Museum (bought in 1928), Inv. No. T.37–1928, Neg. No. M.274, M.275 (detail).

PLATE 47. SHAWL: loom-woven, Paisley, *c.* 1820.
Warp and weft: cotton warp and wool weft.
Weave: 3×1 warp twill, with 80 warps to the inch.
Size: L. 8 ft. 2½ in. W. 3 ft. 11½ in.
Colours: rifle green, neyron rose, satinwood, forget-me-not, juniper, Post Office red, on a cream ground. B.C.C. Nos. 27, 35, 65, 84, 192, 209, and 3.
Collection: Paisley Museum, Ref. No. 52b/42.

PLATE 49. SHAWL: loom-woven, Paisley, c. 1860.
Warp and weft: silk warp and goat-fleece weft.
Weave: 3×1 twill, with 85 warps to the inch.
Size: L. 11 ft. 10 in. W. 5 ft. 4 in.
Colours: pink, red, orange, yellow, two blues and white.
Collection: Wm. Macintyre Esq, c/o Messrs Robert Cochran & Sons Ltd, Paisley.

PLATE 50. SHAWL: loom-woven, Paisley, c. 1850.
Warp and weft: wool warp and weft. 3-in. border of silk warps at each side.
Weave: 3×1 twill, with 104 warps to the inch.
Size: L. 11 ft. 4 in. W. 5 ft. 1½ in.
Colours: apple green, rose pink, peony red, tangerine, Cossack green, turquoise blue, cardinal, jet black, on a cream ground. B.C.C. Nos. 22, 32, 37, 55, 105, 118, 186, 220, and 3.
Collection: Property of R. Cruickshank, 2 Chester Street, Edinburgh, 3.

PLATE 51. SHAWL: loom-woven, Paisley, c. 1865.
Warp and weft: silk warps and woollen wefts. (Analysed by the Shirley Institute, Manchester).
Weave: 3×1 twill, with 100 warps to the inch.
Size: L. 11 ft. 5 in. W. 5 ft. 3½ in.
Colours: red, pink, yellow, blue, green, black and white.

Collection: Wm. Macintyre Esq, c/o Messrs Robert Cochran & Sons Ltd, Paisley.

PLATE 52. SHAWL: loom-woven, Kashmir, mid-19th century, backed and used as a curtain.
Warp and weft: goat-fleece.
Weave: 2×2 twill, with 96 warps to the inch.
Size: L. 10 ft. 2 in. W. 4 ft. 6 in. Height of large cones, 2 ft. 3 in.
Colours: (dark) malmaison rose, claret, peony red, ruby, straw, green muscat, sky green, cardinal, jet black, with centre ground ecru, pattern warp cardinal and narrow border banana. B.C.C. Nos. 16, 36, 37, 38, 51, 76, 161, 186, 220 with 63, 168 and 64.
Collection: Victoria and Albert Museum (given by H.H. The Maharaja Bahadur Sir Prodyot Coomar Tagore in 1933). Inv. No. I.M.14–1933, Neg. No. M.283.

PLATE 53. REVERSIBLE SHAWL: loom-woven, Paisley, c. 1870.
Warp and weft: warps, cotton with silk; wefts, silk, wool, cotton and cotton with silk.
Weave: plain weave, with 54 warps to the inch.
Size: L. 5 ft. 8 in. W. 5 ft. 4 in.
Colours: nigger brown, bunting yellow, turquoise green, guardsman red, stone white with warps of cardinal. B.C.C. Nos. 20, 113, 121, 128, 61, and 186.
Collection: Victoria and Albert Museum (bought in 1928), Inv. No. T.38–1928, Neg. No. M.401.

INDEX

Maharajah Gulab Singh, 9, 28
Manrique, Sebastien, 9, 10
Manucci, Niccolao, 5
'map-shawls' (Kashmir), 14 and n.
Marie Louise (see Empress Marie Louise)
Maze-Sencier, Alphonse, 33
Millar & Sons, Paisley shawl merchants, 28, 29
Mohkuns, or shawl-brokers (Kashmir), 8
'moon-shawls' (Kashmir), 15
Moorcroft, William, Chapter I *passim*; his residence
  in Kashmir, 6; his acquaintance with John Hunter,
  26; his departure for India, 27
Museum of Fine Arts, Boston, 56, 58, and plates 4-5,
  12-15

Napoleon, 32, 33
Naqqāsh, or pattern-drawer (Kashmir), 7, and illus.
  no. 2
Needleworked shawls (see *'Amli*)
Norwich shawls, 19-22, 25n., 32; prices 21, com-
  petition with Paisley, 21

Paisley Museum, 31, 35, 63, and plates 42-43, 47
Paisley shawls, Chapter II *passim*; French designs
  pirated, 35-36; Norwich designs pirated, 21;
  prices, 24, 36
Pashmina, 5
'patent double-shawl' (Paisley), 31
Patent Office, London, 21, 63, and plates 44-45
Pattern-drawer: in Kashmir, 7; Paisley, 30; to be
  brought from Kashmir to U.K., 46-48
Pelsaert, Francisco, 9
Persia, produces Kashmir imitations, 12, 17
Phīri, or seconds wool, 6
Plaid shawls (Paisley), 31, 35
Poll-tax, on Kashmir weavers, 9
Powis (see *Countess of*)

Queen Victoria, receives Kashmir shawls as tribute,
  28
Qutb-Shah of Golconda, 11, and illus. no. 1

Racinet, Auguste, 33
Rafugar, or embroiderer (Kashmir), 3-4
Ranjit Singh, Sikh ruler, 4, 14
Rémusat, Mme de, 32

Reversible shawls: from Kashmir, 17; from Paisley
  35-36
Rey, J., 15, 33
'ring-shawls', 5
Rivière, Mme, 15, and illus. no. 5
Roe, Sir Thomas, 10
Royal Society, 19, 26
Royal Scottish Museum, Edinburgh, 59, and plate 19
Rutherford, George, 25

Shāl-cloth, exported to Europe in 17th century, 19
Shāl, defined, 2
Shawl-goat, attempts to naturalize in Europe, 25-28
Sime & Son, David, Edinburgh shawl merchants, 23
Simpson, William, 16
Sinclair, Sir John, 26
Society for Improvement of British Wool, Edin-
  burgh, 26
Society of Arts, London, 20, 27, 28
Spinners, in Kashmir, 6
Srinagar, map of, embroidered on shawls, 14 and n.
Sterne, Laurence, 19
Stewart, A. M., 31n., 51

Ta'līm, or weaving-code, 7, and illus. no. 4
Tarah-gurū, or colour-caller, 7
Ternaux, M. Guillaume Louis, 27-28, 34
Tessier, M., 14, 27
Thévenot, Jean de, 11
'Thibet shawls' (Paisley), 29
Thorp, R., 9
Tibet, source of shawl-wool, 5, 6, 25, 27
Tilikar, or loom-woven shawls (Kashmir), 3
Tojli, or spool, 3, 7
Turner, Captain Samuel, 26
Twill-tapestry technique, 3, 8

Ustād, or loom-owner (Kashmir), 7-8

Victoria, (see *Queen Victoria*)
Vigne, G. T., 5, 7, 14

Warner, Sir Frank, 19
Wilson, H. H., 26
Wilson, John, 23

Yūsuf, Khwāja, 4, 14 (*see under* 'K')

Zain-ul-'Abidīn, 2

THE PLATES

PLATE 1. Fragment of shawl: loom-woven, Kashmir, *c.* 1680

PLATE 2. Fragment of shawl:
loom-woven, Kashmir, early
eighteenth century

PLATE 3. Fragment of shawl: loom-woven, Kashmir, first half
of the eighteenth century

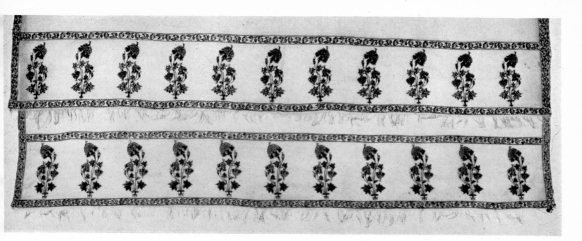

PLATE 4. End-borders of a shawl: loom-woven, Kashmir, early eighteenth century

PLATE 5. Detail of Plate 4

PLATE 6. Fragment of shawl: loom-woven, Kashmir, mid-eighteenth century

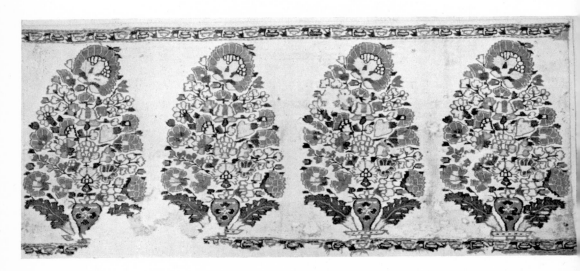

PLATE 7. Fragment of shawl: loom-woven, Kashmir, mid-eighteenth century

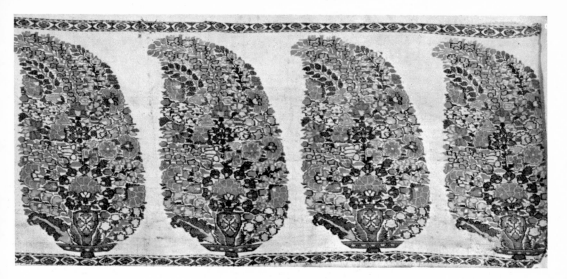

PLATE 8. Fragment of shawl: loom-woven, Kashmir, second half of the eighteenth century

PLATE 9. Detail of a shawl: loom-woven, Kashmir, second half of the eighteenth century

PLATE 10. Fragment of cloth: loom–woven, probably Kirman, Persia, late eighteenth century

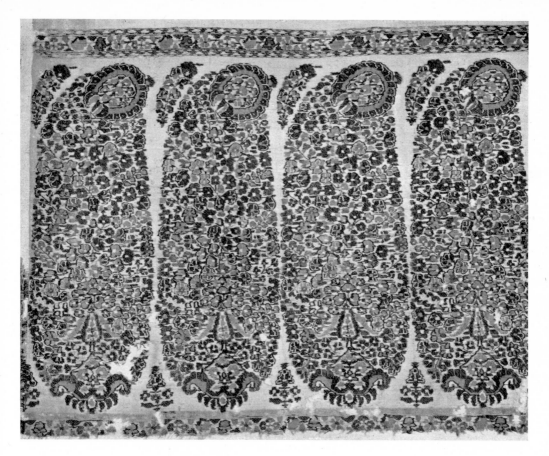

PLATE 11. Fragment of shawl: loom-woven, Kashmir, late eighteenth century

PLATE 12. Piece of shawl-cloth: loom-woven, Kashmir, late eighteenth or early nineteenth century

PLATE 13. Piece of shawl-cloth: loom-woven, Kashmir, late eighteenth or early nineteenth century

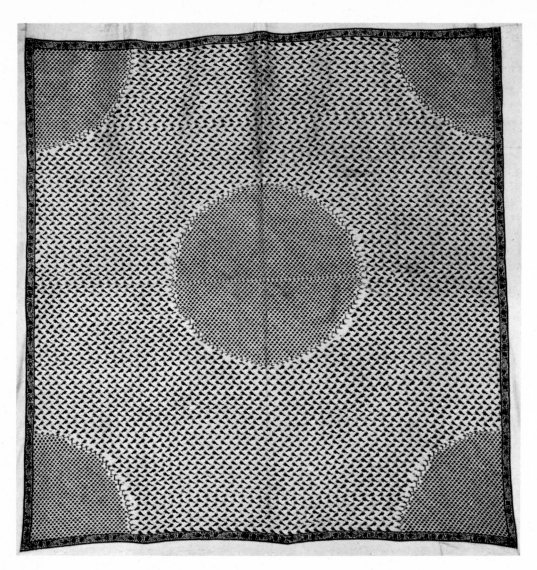

PLATE 14. Shawl: loom-woven. Kashmir, early nineteenth century

PLATE 15. Detail of shawl at Plate 14

PLATE 16. Detail of shawl: loom-woven, Kashmir, *c*. 1800

PLATE 17. Detail of shawl: loom-woven, Kashmir, *c.* 1800

PLATE 18. Girdle: loom-woven, Kashmir, second quarter of nineteenth century

PLATE 19. Part of a girdle: loom-woven, Kashmir, late eighteenth or early
nineteenth century

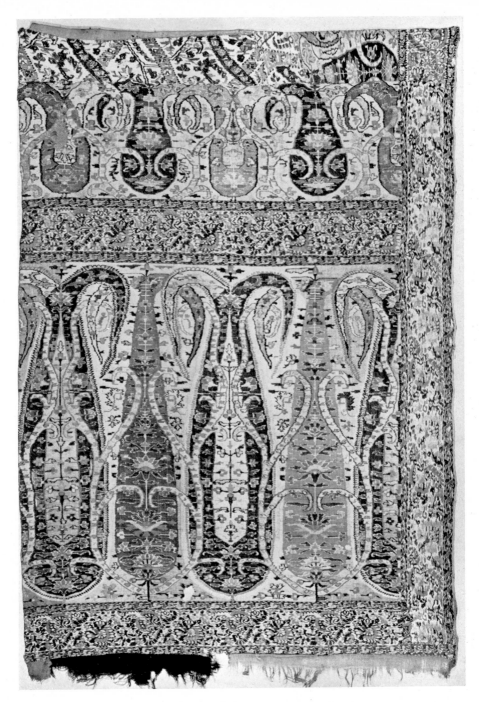

PLATE 20. Part of a shawl: loom-woven, Kashmir, *c.* 1820

PLATE 21. Part of a shawl: loom-woven, Kashmir, *c.* 1820

PLATE 22. Scarf or girdle: embroidered with a needle, Kashmir, *c.* 1830

PLATE 23. Scarf or girdle: embroidered with a needle, Kashmir, *c.* 1840

PLATE 24. Scarf or girdle: embroidered with a needle, possibly Punjab, *c.* 1860

PLATE 25. Part of a shawl: loom-woven, Kashmir, *c.* 1820

PLATE 26. Part of a shawl: loom-woven, Kashmir, *c.* 1830

PLATE 27. Part of a shawl: loom-woven, Kashmir, *c*. 1830

PLATE 28. Part of a shawl: loom-woven, Kashmir, *c.* 1825

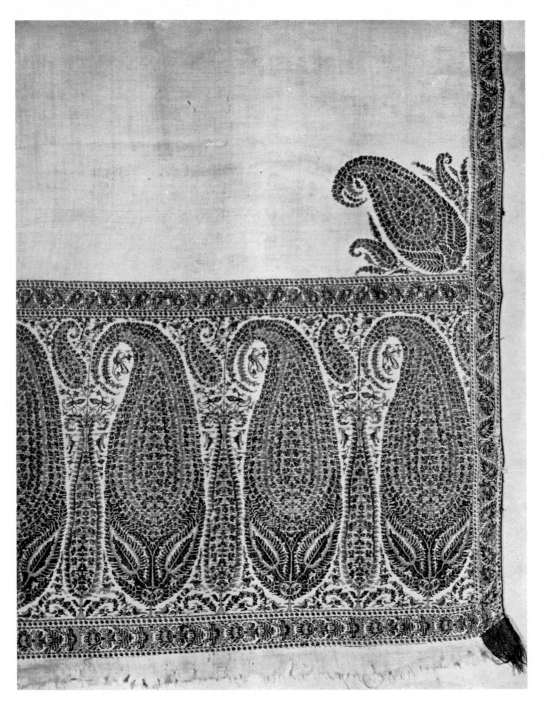

PLATE 29. Part of a shawl: loom-woven, Kashmir, *c.* 1830

PLATE 30. Detail of shawl: loom-woven, Kashmir, c. 1830

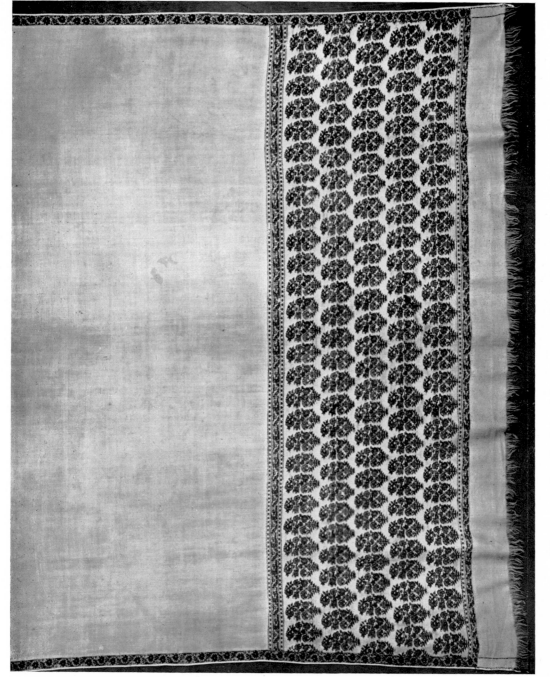

PLATE 31. Detail of shawl: loom-woven, Kashmir, early nineteenth century

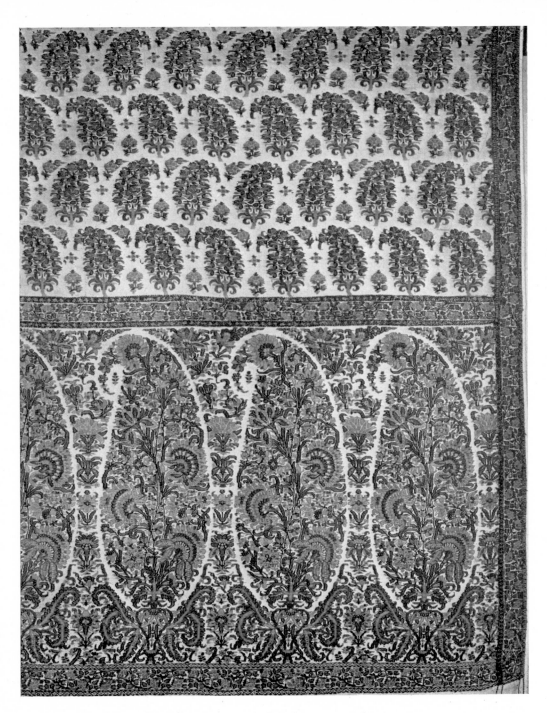

PLATE 32. Detail of shawl: loom-woven, Kashmir, *c.* 1830

PLATE 33. Scarf or girdle: reversible weave, Kashmir, 1865

PLATE 34. Man's coat: loom-woven, Kashmir, early nineteenth century

PLATE 35.   Detail of shawl: loom-woven (patchwork construction), Kashmir, *c.* 1870

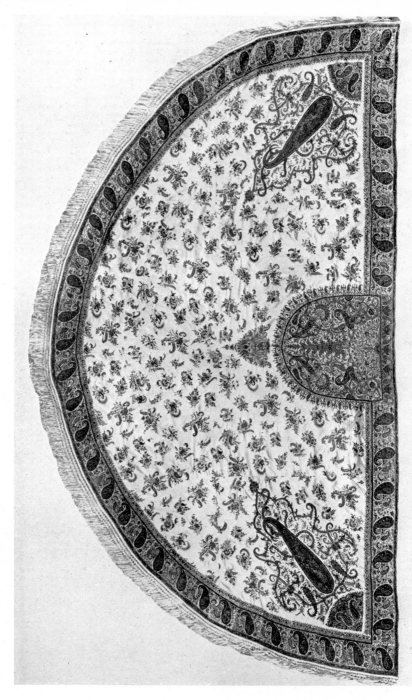

PLATE 36. Shawl: embroidered with a needle, probably Persian,
mid–nineteenth century

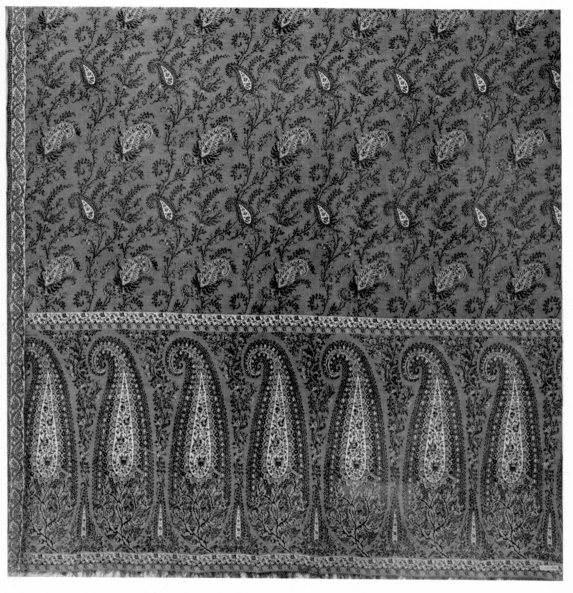

PLATE 37. Detail of shawl: loom-woven, Norwich, *c.* 1835

PLATE 38. Detail of shawl: loom-woven, Norwich, *c.* 1835

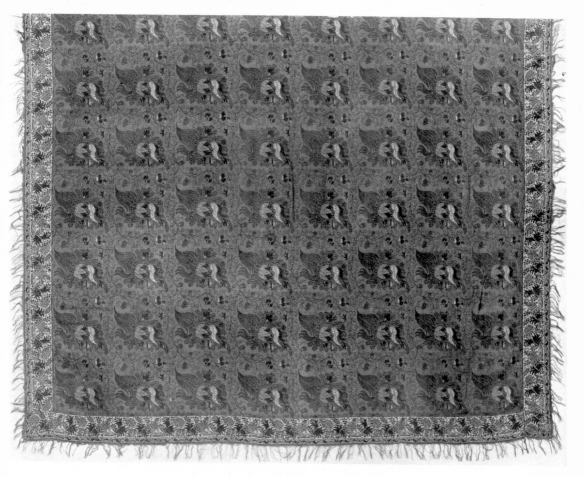

PLATE 39. Shawl: loom-woven, Norwich, *c.* 1835

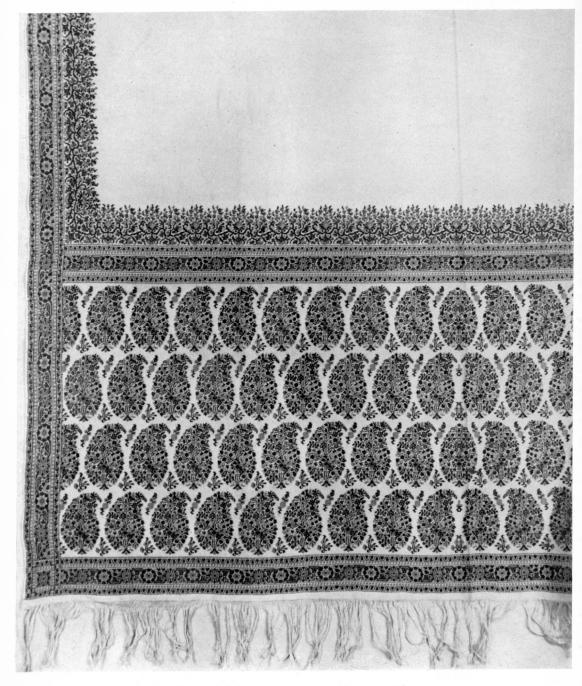

PLATE 40. Shawl: loom-woven, possibly Norwich, *c.* 1860

PLATE 41. Shawl: loom-woven, Norwich, mid-nineteenth century

PLATE 42. Detail of square shawl: loom-woven, Norwich, *c.* 1830

PLATE 43. Detail of square shawl: loom-woven, Paisley, *c.* 1825

PLATE 44. Sample of shawl-fabric: loom-woven, Edinburgh, 1843
(Registered at the Patents Office in this year)

PLATE 45. Sample of shawl-fabric: loom-woven, Norwich, 1843
(Registered at the Patents Office in this year)

P

PLATE 46. Close-up of fake Persian inscription
appearing in the centre of the Paisley shawl at
Plate 48

PLATE 47. Detail of shawl: loom-woven, Paisley, *c.* 1820

PLATE 48. Shawl: loom-woven, Paisley, *c.* 1865

PLATE 49. Shawl: loom-woven, Paisley, *c.* 1860

PLATE 50. Shawl: loom-woven, Paisley, *c.* 1850

PLATE 51. Shawl: loom-woven, Paisley, *c.* 1865

PLATE 52. Shawl: loom-woven, Kashmir, *c.* 1860

PLATE 53. Reversible shawl: loom-woven, Paisley, *c.* 1870